# PLEASE TELL ME . . .

**Questions People Ask about Freemasonry—and the Answers**

BY **Tom C. McKenney**
Author of *The Deadly Deception*

FOREWORD BY EVANS CRARY, JR., 33°
KNIGHT TEMPLAR, PAST GRAND MASTER,
GRAND LODGE OF FLORIDA

Huntington House Publishers

Huntington House Publishers
P.O. Box 53788
Lafayette, Louisiana 70505

Library of Congress Card Catalog Number 94-75443
ISBN 1-56384-013-8

Printed in the U.S.A.

All Scripture quotations are taken
from the King James Version of the Bible.
In all quotations from Masonic sources,
words within parentheses are for clarification
and are my own.

**Cover by Joe McCormick**

# Dedication

To Jim Shaw, who loved Freemasonry with all his heart, pursued its knowledge and served its institutions with all his mind and strength, and who, unlike the rich, young ruler, forsook it all to follow Jesus, and has never looked back. For the remainder of his life, he has quietly given all that he has to reach other Masons with the truth that set him free.

And for Bonnie, his wife, who has walked with Jim every painful, dangerous step of the way, paying with him the price of massive rejection and all the years of fear and persecution.

# Contents

# Preface

*Am I therefore become your enemy, because I tell you the truth?*

—Galatians 4:16

This book is not "anti-Masonic"; this book is simply the truth—spoken, I pray, in love. I have lived some things, learned some things that most Masons don't know—things that they need to know—and have attempted to set them down in an orderly way as honestly and simply as I can. I am not the enemy of Masons. I am their friend, their advocate, seeking to tell them the truth about the system that deceives them, uses them, and tramples on their loyalty. What I oppose is that system.

Many, many times, at the end of a talk-show interview, I have been asked, "Tom, what one last thing would you like to say?" My reply is always the same: To the non-Mason, and especially the potential Mason, I say, "Please learn the facts, arm yourself with the truth." To the Mason, if he will listen to just one thing I say, it is, "Don't be afraid of the truth; Jesus promised that if we give it a chance, the truth will set us free." And, I say this to you now. Don't be afraid of the truth; it is only the lie that can hurt you.

# Foreword

Dear Reader,

I labored diligently in the halls of Freemasonry for twenty years, attained its highest honors and enjoyed Masonic fellowship with men of the highest integrity and good morals; but, I did not find true peace and happiness until I met Jesus Christ as my personal savior and baptizer in the Holy Spirit in the spring of 1975. From the moment that I was "Born Again" until now, I have experienced the truth of Jesus' words, "I am the way, the truth and the life, no man comes unto the Father but by me" and have discovered that His truth and His word are indeed the liberating, empowering presence that men have sought since the beginning.

Tom C. McKenney has labored diligently to investigate and chronical the foundations, teachings, and theological roots of Freemasonry and has presented them in this book in a thoughtful, powerful, and logical way to the consideration of those who are truly seeking further light for their lives and those of their loved ones. The inescapable conclusion is that Jesus is the only way to the Father and that all other ways lead to darkness and death.

Having walked the wrong way for so long a time, I know from personal experience that "there are none so blind as those who will not see." I commend this work to you, the reader, in the hope that your eyes will be opened to the truth and light of Jesus Christ as the only way to the abundant life both now and forever.

> Your faithful servant in Jesus,
> Evans Crary, Jr.

# Introduction

*To the law and to the testimony: if they speak not according to this Word, it is because there is no light in them.*

—Isaiah 8:20

For twenty years, I have studied Freemasonry, the Masonic Lodge system that encircles the globe and permeates America, with threads reaching into the fabric of virtually every social, religious, and political institution in the nation—even the church. My entering into this study was sudden. The thought of doing such a thing had never previously crossed my mind.

It all began for me one night in Kentucky with a little blue book. At the time, my family and I were trying to help a young man put the broken pieces of his life together by bringing him to the Lord. He came to see us one night with a small, blue book in his hand and a mysterious air about him.

"Man," he said with a mixture of excitement and awe in his voice, "I've got a secret book here. I found it in my grandfather's attic. It's a Mason's book, and I'm not even supposed to see it. But, I've been reading it, and there's some very heavy stuff in here." He wanted me to read the book, and I didn't want to, not at all. But, to please him, because he was so spiritually fragile, I promised to read at least the introduction. I did, and it literally changed my life, for it launched me into a twenty-year study of Freemasonry and its complex system of organizations and degrees, a study that will probably go on for the rest of my life.

Prior to that night, I never had even the slightest interest in Freemasonry. My father had been a York Rite Mason and a Shriner, but he was completely inactive, never went to meetings, and never once spoke of it. Because of my promise to our struggling young friend and despite my disinterest, I began, reluctantly, to read the introduction.

I was not long into the introduction before I read the author's very plain statement that Freemasonry is a modern day revival of the pagan mystery religions of antiquity, especially those practiced in the temples of Isis and Osiris in Egypt. This amazed me! I had always thought (if I thought of it at all) that the Masons were the "gung ho" of Protestantism, as opposed to the Knights of Columbus, who were the "gung ho" of Catholicism. This man was saying something radically different!

Then, the author went on to say that Jesus was not unique, that He was just one of many great religious leaders of the past. He said that every great civilization has had its myth of a messiah, typically believed to have been born of a virgin, a worker of miracles, put to death by wicked men, and raised from the dead. This, of course, gripped my attention, for Jesus is either everything that He claimed to be, the unique redeemer of lost mankind, the only way for sinful man to be reconciled to the Father in Heaven, or He is a dead phony. (He can't be something in between these possibilities, for He plainly declared Himself to be divine, the unique Savior of lost and sinful mankind [John 14:6, et al.].) Still, nothing prepared me for the statement on the next page, which swept me into the pursuit of the truth concerning all this.

The Masonic author listed the messiahs of various civilizations and then concluded with a statement that nearly knocked me off the chair! The Hindu messiah, he said, is Krishna; the Christian's messiah is Jesus; and the Mason's messiah is Hiram. "Hiram!" I exclaimed. "If the Mason's messiah is not Jesus, but is instead some guy named Hiram, I want to know who this Hiram is!"

Since that day twenty years ago, I have traveled hundreds of thousands of miles, read dozens of books, and consulted with dozens of other students of Masonry, both Christian and non-Christian. Beginning with that little blue book, I have accumulated a personal library of more than one hundred Masonic reference works, all allegedly secret, and all of which I am "not supposed to have." Since writing my own book on Freemasonry, *The Deadly Deception*, I have appeared on nearly three hundred radio and television talk shows all over the United States and Canada, answering thousands of callers' questions. Some of the questions have been hostile, and some irrelevant, but most have been sincere inquiries from sincere people who want very much to know what Freemasonry is, what Masons believe and do, and what it is that their loved ones are involved in. They want to know what goes on behind the closed and guarded doors in those mysterious, windowless buildings.

Over the five years of traveling, speaking, and listening since the release of *The Deadly Deception*, I have noticed two interesting things. First, there seems to be no end to the interest in this subject. Although it seems to me that the nation should by now have been saturated with the truth about Freemasonry, the demand for my appearances on talk shows continues undiminished, and on each one the listeners react as if it were a brand new topic! Second, I have been asked many of the same questions repeatedly, prefaced by the plea, "Please tell me. . . ."

This book contains those most repeated, most important questions and the answers, taken from the very best Masonic sources. Concerning Masonic doctrine, rituals, and practices, not one Christian book is referenced here; I have allowed the Masonic authorities to speak for themselves. There are also, in the back of the book, appendices containing more in-depth information about some of the most important (and most controversial) aspects of Masonry. These, like the answers in the book itself, are carefully documented and based on the very best Masonic authorities and historical sources. According to Freemasonry's own authorities, here are the answers to the questions.

# 1

# The Nature and Origins of Freemasonry

*For they have sown the wind, and they shall reap the whirl-wind.*

—Hosea 8:7

## 1. What is Freemasonry?

Freemasonry, according to the *Encyclopaedia Britannica*, is the world's largest secret society. It is a fraternal order, for "freeborn" white men, "sound of limb" (not blind, deaf, or crippled), of age twenty-one or older, binding its initiates to one another and to the institution, for life, by death oaths.[1]

## 2. Why the *free* in Freemasonry?

I have deliberately called the society *Freemasonry* here at the beginning because it is the correct term, and because many people, knowing little or nothing of the institution, may think we're speaking of bricklayers when hearing just *Masonry*.

Different Masons may give you different answers here (and each will believe that he is right), but the most generally accepted answer is the following. The *free* part of the name comes from the symbolism of the medieval stone-masonry guilds in which, once a man had advanced to the status of a master mason, he worked for himself and was "free" to travel over the land practicing his trade without supervision.

However, in Masonic speech the terms *Mason* and *Freemason* are synonymous and will be used as such throughout the remainder of this book.

## 3. In what way is it secret?

Although its existence is not a secret, its rituals, handshakes, passwords, recognition signs, penalty signs, and death oaths (what they call "the secret work") are supposedly secret. Their meetings are held behind guarded doors, in buildings with no windows (or with the windows painted over or heavily curtained). One condition of their binding death oaths is never to reveal any of the "secret work" to a non-Mason (or a Mason who has not been initiated into that particular degree).

## 4. Where and when did Freemasonry begin?

You will get different answers to this question from different Masonic sources. Most Masons will tell you that it had its beginnings in the building of the first temple in Jerusalem by King Solomon. Others will claim that its origins are even more ancient, with a few who will tell you that it goes clear back to Adam in the Garden of Eden. Serious Masonic scholars, however, laugh at such claims.[2]

The fact is that Freemasonry, as we know it, had its beginnings in eighteenth century England. The first recorded meeting was held in London in the Goose and Gridiron Tavern, 24 June 1717, to form the Grand Lodge of England. Most early meetings of English lodges were held in taverns.

## 5. How did it happen?

It seems to have begun because educated men with time on their hands were looking for a social and intellectual distraction, apparently never dreaming that it would eventually develop into what it has become. (Interestingly, the same is true of the origin of the Ku Klux Klan.)

Although there seems to be no reliable record, Masonic tradition has it that two men, James Anderson, D.D., and the Reverend John Desaguliers, scientist, philosopher, and third Grand Master, took the pagan mystery religions of Egypt, especially the worship of Isis and Osiris, reduced them to degree form, and created the first three degrees of Masonry. Much of their symbolism was borrowed from the medieval stonemason guilds and the biblical account of the building of Solomon's Temple. The work of Anderson and Desaguliers was improved upon, added to, and revised by others so that by the late eighteenth century these first three degrees were in final form, very much as they are today.

The secrecy and the exclusivity of the membership apparently appealed to British gentlemen of means. Prominent men were attracted, and the lodges duplicated rapidly, spreading first to the other British Isles, then to Europe and the American colonies.

This summary of Freemasonry's beginnings is necessarily abbreviated and, therefore, imperfect; but for our purposes it must suffice.[3]

## 6. But, why do they call themselves *Masons*, if they don't lay brick or stone?

They refer to what they do as "speculative" (symbolic) Masonry, as opposed to laboring as masons building things with bricks, blocks, or stone, which they call "operative" masonry. In the beginning, it was an organization for educated gentlemen of means, something of a philosophical society with the symbolism of a stonemason's trade. There were no "operative" masons in the order. Today, of course, there are some working masons who are also "speculative" Masons, members of the Masonic Lodge.

## 7. Do you mean that Masonry has something to do with Egyptian pagan religions?

Masonry has everything to do with Egyptian pagan religions. With no exception, the Masonic philosophers and writers of doctrine trace Freemasonry directly back to the mystery religions of the East, especially those of Isis and Osiris of Egypt. Agreeing with Albert Pike and Joseph Fort Newton, two of Masonry's most respected authorities, *The Kentucky Monitor* declares plainly, "Freemasonry has come to us from the Ancient Mysteries of Osiris and Isis as celebrated in Egypt; that we owe much of our ritual to those old systems, and that from them and through them to even more remote sources we trace much of our doctrine."[4]

According to the consensus of Masonic authorities, the only pure form of religion that ever existed was that of the ancient pagan mysteries, and they were adulterated, contaminated, and forgotten by Hebrews and then Christians through the ages. Masonry, they teach, is a revival of those pagan mystery religions, an effort to rediscover their secrets and restore their perfection. J.D. Buck, in his book *Mystic Masonry*, expresses it this way:

> Drop the theological barnacles from the Religion of Jesus, as taught by Him, and by the Essenes and Gnostics of the first centuries, and it becomes Masonry. Masonry in its purity, derived as it is from the old Hebrew Kabalah as part of the Great Universal Wisdom Religion of remotest antiquity . . .[5]

Their goal is that, through study and meditation, the mysteries will be restored to their ancient perfection and all men will gather to worship the nature gods and goddesses at only one altar, the altar of Masonry. Again, *The Kentucky Monitor* is clear:

> It [Freemasonry] makes no pretense of Christianity, and wars not against sectarian creeds or doctrines, but looks forward to the time when the labor of our ancient brethren shall be symbolized by the erection of a spiritual temple (worthy of) civilization. A temple in which there shall be one altar and but one worship, one common altar of Masonry . . .[6]

## 8. How and when did Masonry come to the United States?

All the early American lodges were chartered by the Grand Lodge of England. Here again, Masonic historians make different claims about which lodge was the first established in the colonies. The generally accepted version is that the first American lodge was established in 1730 in Boston, and the second in 1733 in Philadelphia. This first lodge in Philadelphia, of which Benjamin Franklin was an early member, met at Tun Tavern, also the site of the first recruitment of American marines in 1775 and considered to be the birthplace of the U.S. Marine Corps.

## 9. Why all the symbolic references to building?

The symbolic references to building have to do with the goal of self-improvement and character building in the members. They teach that the individual Mason, by his lessons in religion and morality and by his association with other Masons, is gradually perfected, both socially and spiritually. They proudly proclaim, "We make good men better" (which, significantly, makes no provision for making bad men good).

## Endnotes

1. *The New Encyclopaedia Britannica*, 15th ed., s.v. "Freemasonry"; Malcolm C. Duncan, *Duncan's Masonic Ritual and Monitor*, 3rd ed. (New York: David McKay Co., Inc.), 29, 34, 35, 64-66, 94-96; see chapter 12, "Masonry's Exclusiveness and Elitism."

2. Those who really believe this probably also believe in Santa Claus, the Tooth Fairy, and the essential goodness of man. "Even Blue Masonry cannot trace back its authentic history, with its present degrees, further than the year 1700, if so far," wrote Albert Pike in *Morals and Dogma,* rev. ed. (Washington, DC: House of the Temple, 1950), 208.

3. As is the case with much of Masonic doctrine, the authorities differ, with about as many "factual" accounts as there are writ-

ers, often in contradiction with one another. To pursue the subject seriously is to experience frustration and confusion.

4. Henry Pirtle, *The Kentucky Monitor,* 9th ed. (Louisville, KY: Standard Printing Co., 1921), xi, xii.

5. J.D. Buck, *Mystic Masonry,* 3rd ed. (Chicago: Chas T. Powner Co., 1925), 66, 67.

6. Pirtle, *The Kentucky Monitor,* 95.

# 2

# The Scope of Masonry

*A little leaven leaveneth the whole lump.*

—Galatians 5:9

## 1. Is Masonry found only in England and the United States?

Freemasonry is worldwide, with lodges in every major nation except for Iran. The Ayatollah Khomeini closed the Iranian lodges after the shah was deposed. Until recent years, there were no lodges in China or Cuba, but lodges are now reopened in both. Although the majority of Masons are in the United States, there are lodges around the world, with rituals largely the same.

## 2. In what other countries is Masonry strong?

Masonry is strongest in Great Britain, where it originated. In the Grand Lodge of England, the position of Grand Master is usually held by a member of the Royal Family. Masonry is also very strong in Western Europe and Scandinavia, where royalty also often rule in the Lodge. In France, Masonry has tended to be a political force and is considered a "rogue" branch of Masonry with very strong leanings toward the occult.

## 3. Is Masonry powerful in the United States?

Yes, it is, especially in some regions and in some social, political, and religious settings. For example, there are some places where one cannot be hired if not a Mason; elsewhere, promotions depend on the man's being a Mason. A man in Indiana related to the federal government that in eleven years of work with his employer, he had been denied promotion eight times because he refuses to join the Masonic Lodge. Masonry tends to be strong in police departments, and this creates problems in terms of fair and objective enforcement of the law. In Maryland, for example, automobile license plates have distinctive prefixes for Masons; since many, if not most, policemen are Masons, the problem is obvious.

## 4. How many Masons are there?

No one but God really knows the answer to this question (with the exception, perhaps, of Satan) because there is no single, overall headquarters to keep track. Although the various grand lodges around the world cooperate and are networked, each tends to be autonomous with no one man or group in control of them all. However, the best estimates are that there are between two and three million Masons in the United States and another one million in the rest of the world.

## 5. Are the Masons' numbers going up or down?

Masonic membership in the United States is in a steep decline; numbers are dropping, and with much fewer young men entering the Lodge, the average age is going up. According to the *Scottish Rite Journal*, Masonry's most prominent and authoritative periodical, the average age of American Masons is estimated at seventy.[1] According to a report presented at the 1990 Conference of Grand Masters of Masons in North America, 40 percent of all Masons are over age sixty-five (compared with the general population of adult white males, where only 5 percent are over sixty-five). The same study estimates that overall membership will drop by 50 percent by the year 2000 and by an additional 50 percent by the year 2010.[2] At this rate, American Masonry would virtually cease to exist within the next thirty or forty years.

## 6. If numbers are declining, why is Masonry still a powerful force in the United States?

Despite the above figures, the lodge system is still a very powerful force in this country. The reason for this is that Masons still occupy positions of power and influence in the legal and judicial system, in local, state, and national government, law enforcement, business, certain parts of the armed forces, and in the churches.

In April 1993, a part of the U.S. Capitol Building was taken over for a day by the Supreme Council of the Thirty-third Degree. It was declared a Masonic Lodge and "tiled" (cleared of all non-Scottish Rite Masons), and George M. White, architect of the United States Capitol, was made a Thirty-second Degree Mason. Do you think your civic group, club, or church could do that? Don't bother to try.

The power of Masonry in the churches was brought out in the open in the conflict within the Southern Baptist Convention during 1992 and 1993. Although the convention admitted, on the record, that there are things about Masonry which are pagan, unscriptural, and in conflict with basic Christian beliefs, the delegates in June 1993 voted ten to one to compromise on the issue and take no stand against it.

## 7. If Masonry is in such a serious decline in numbers, why is it that so many powerful politicians and other prominent men are Masons?

The original members of English Masonry were aristocrats, and they quickly took in members of the royal family. Since "success begets success," politicians and other prominent people have been attracted to it ever since. An organization which can boast "important" men, past and present, readily attracts still more "important" men, and this success perpetuates itself. Even though fewer and fewer "ordinary" men are joining the Lodge, it still attracts the prominent and powerful (and those who seek to be). There are fewer and fewer "Indians" but plenty of "chiefs."

## 8. Is Masonry stronger in some parts of the country than in others?

Definitely—although lodges are to be found in all states, territories, and the District of Columbia, Masonry tends to be much stronger in some parts of the country. Numbers of Masons are greater, and their influence stronger, in the South and Midwest, and much less so in the Northeast and Far West. There are places in the South where a man can't be elected dogcatcher if he is not a Mason.

---

## Endnotes

1. Thomas M. Boles, 33°, "Where Do You Do Your Shopping?," *Scottish Rite Journal* (July 1993): 53.

2. S. Brent Morris, 33°, "Unite in the Grand Design," *Scottish Rite Journal* (May 1990): 46-49.

# 3

# American Masonry: The Blue Lodge and the Higher Degrees

*For a good tree bringeth not forth corrupt fruit; neither doth a corrupt tree bring forth good fruit.*

—Luke 6:43

## 1. How is American Masonry organized?

American Masonry is a rather complex structure built on a broad foundation—the local lodge, referred to by Masons as the Blue Lodge. This is the lodge in your home town. In the South and Midwest, there is likely to be one in even the tiniest of towns. Further, in the South, if there are only three buildings in town besides the general store, they will probably be the Baptist church, the Methodist. church, and the Masonic Lodge. In the local lodge (the Blue Lodge), the first ("Entered Apprentice"), second ("Fellow Craft"), and third ("Master Mason") degrees are conferred and practiced. The third, or Master Mason Degree, is as far as most Masons go, meaning that their entire Masonic experience is limited to the local lodge and its three degrees. Approximately 97 percent go no further.

Built upon the foundation of the local lodge are the higher degrees, the Shrine, all the special Masonic bodies, and the auxiliary groups for women, boys, and girls.[1]

## 2. What is the significance of the *Blue* in Blue Lodge?

This is a hazy area, even among Masonic writers, but it seems to derive from the significance of the sky overhead, and this in two ways. The tradition is that the ancient stonemasons' guilds met on hilltops under the "starry canopy of the Heavens," so many Blue Lodges have blue ceilings (some with stars scattered about); some even have blue doors. Another reason for the "blue heaven" symbolism is that astrology is very important to Masonic doctrine. Additionally, the "ancient brethren" worshiped the heavens, especially the sun, from the highest hills—thus the blue sky and its starry host.[2]

Similarly, lodge halls are often above the ground floor, the custom descending from "high place" worship as well as for enhanced security. Daniel Sickles, venerable Masonic authority, explains: "Lodge meetings at the present day are usually held in upper chambers. Before the erection of Temples the celestial bodies [stars and planets] were worshipped on hills, and the terrestrial ones [Earth spirits] in the valleys."[3] *The Kentucky Monitor* adds, "It may be, however, that the custom had its origin in a practice observed by the ancient Jews (of worshiping in the highest places)."[4]

## 3. What are the "higher degrees"?

As Freemasonry evolved, systems of additional degrees were conceived, and, to varying degrees, Masons accepted, embraced, and joined them. The basic concept was (and is) that there should be further steps toward perfection than were found in the original three degrees. An additional factor contributing to their development and acceptance is the elitist appeal of becoming one of the relative few who occupy higher positions than the rest.

In Freemasonry's early days, some systems of higher degrees failed to attract wide acceptance and died on the vine, while others grew. Since "success begets success," those degree systems which attracted more men tended then to attract still more (People love to join "the best."), and some prospered while others withered and died.

To make the matter even more complex, some individual degrees in the "higher" systems attracted such a following that separate chapters were organized. The best example of this is the Royal Arch degree, the seventh degree of the York Rite, which has become a separate organization within the overall system, with its own books of ritual and doctrine, officers, regular meetings, dues, etc. It is interesting to me that the Royal Arch degree claims to be a "Christian" degree but is, in fact, probably the most wicked of earned degrees. (See chapter 4, "Masonry's 'Christian' Degrees.")

## 4. What are the systems for the "higher degrees" in America?

In American Masonry, two such systems of higher degrees prevail: the York Rite and the Scottish Rite. By far the larger and more influential of these is the Scottish Rite. The Scottish Rite is further divided into northern and southern jurisdictions. Although they cooperate, neither answers to the other.[5] The Southern Jurisdiction of the Scottish Rite is much larger and more powerful, including all states, territories, and trusts, except for the fourteen Midwest and Northeast states that comprise the Northern Jurisdiction.[6]

## 5. Who can join these systems and earn the higher degrees?

Any Mason, after six months as a Master Mason (third degree), if he has the time and money, may join either the York or Scottish Rite and begin the climb to "the top." In order to remain in the York or Scottish Rite, the man must not only satisfy the requirements of the rite (attendance, dues, etc.) but must also continue to be a Master Mason in good standing in his local Blue Lodge.

## 6. What is the difference between the York Rite and the Scottish Rite?

In the York Rite, the Mason climbs through a total of ten additional degrees, culminating in his becoming a "Knight Templar." He can then sign his name "Hiram A. Mason, KT." In the Scottish Rite, the Mason goes through twenty-nine additional degrees culminating in the Thirty-second Degree ("Sublime Prince of the Royal Secret"). The Thirty-second Degree Mason can then sign his name "John Q. Mason, 32°." The degree of Knight Templar is the equivalent of the Thirty-second Degree, so the two are viewed as being at the same level.

Some Masons, with extra time, money, and motivation, go through both the York and Scottish Rites. Such a man can then sign his name "Mason A. Cuttabuv, KT, 32°."

## 7. Is there a headquarters for Masonry in America?

Since each state and territory is a Grand Lodge, essentially sovereign and independent of the others, there is no single headquarters, nor a central authority recognized by all Masons. Despite this, the House of the Temple, headquarters of the Southern Jurisdiction of the Scottish Rite, seat of the Supreme Council of the Thirty-third Degree, tends to function as such *de facto* because of its size, influence, and power. In fact, this Supreme Council claims to be the "Mother Jurisdiction of the World," and former Sovereign Grand Commander of the Southern Jurisdiction, Albert Pike, took upon himself the title, "Supreme Pontiff of Universal Freemasonry."

---

### Endnotes

1. "Busy, Brotherly World of Freemasonry," *LIFE Magazine* (8 October 1956): 104-122.

2. Albert Pike, *Morals and Dogma*, rev. ed. (Washington, DC: House of the Temple, 1950).

3. Daniel Sickles, *Ahiman Rhezon and Freemason's Guide* (New York: MaCoy Publishing Co., 1911), 75.

4. Henry Pirtle, *The Kentucky Monitor,* 9th ed. (Louisville, KY: Standard Printing Co., 1921), 36,37. Mr. Pirtle is in error here; worshiping on high places was an ancient pagan practice adopted by backsliding Israelites. It did not originate with the Israelites.

5. "Busy, Brotherly World," 104-109.

6. The fourteen states of the Northern Jurisdiction are Illinois, Wisconsin, Indiana, Ohio, Michigan, Pennsylvania, New Jersey, New York, Connecticut, Rhode Island, Massachusetts, Vermont, New Hampshire, and Maine.

For several years, a Masonic lodge and this church were housed in the same building north of Birmingham, Alabama. The shared sign suggests they are one and the same. Notice the Masonic symbols above the sign.

# 4

## Masonry's "Christian" Degrees

*I know thy works, that thou hast a name that thou livest, and art dead.*

—Revelation 3:1

### 1. Are there any Christian degrees in Masonry?

No, at least there are none that answer to the biblical definition of the word "Christian," because they are part of the overall Masonic system with its death oaths and deception. Masonry reduces the Bible to the level of equality with all other "holy books," no better than the Koran or the Hindu Vedas. It denies the uniqueness of Jesus Christ as the sole redeemer of lost mankind (John 14:6) and reduces Him to the status of being merely one of many "exemplars" (great men of the past). There can be nothing truly Christian about any such system; one gallon of ice cream and nine gallons of dirt combine to make ten gallons of very dirty ice cream.

### 2. Do Masons claim to have Christian degrees?

York Rite (also called American Rite) Masons, when confronted with Masonry's obvious paganism, claim that theirs is different from all the rest of Masonry, that theirs is a Christian rite because Christ and Christian symbolism appear in some parts of their ritual. In fact, the degree of Knight Templar, the York Rite's highest degree, is open only to "professing Christians," and, in the ritual, the candidate promises that if he is called upon to "draw his sword in a religious cause," he will "give preference to the Christian religion" (which seems to me to be a strange and watery commitment).

## 3. If York Rite Masons must profess to be Christians in order to receive their highest degree and must mention Christ in their ritual, doesn't that make it a Christian branch of Masonry?

While it is true that Jesus is mentioned in some of the York Rite degrees, the critical issues of man's essential sinfulness and the uniqueness of Jesus as the only means of redemption are never expressed. In only four of the ten degrees is Christ mentioned at all.

## 4. But, since Jesus is mentioned in at least some of their degrees, doesn't this still make the York Rite a Christian organization?

No, it does not, and, again, this is so for at least the following reasons:

a. To make references to Jesus in an organization's rituals and lessons, but as less than what He really is, as less than God the Son, unique Redeemer, the only means of reconciliation for lost and sinful mankind, is not only invalid but blasphemous. We cannot have Jesus Christ on our own terms. A watered-down concept of Jesus is no Jesus at all.

b. Prayers in the York Rite are the Christless "universal" prayers of the rest of Masonry, never prayed in the name of Jesus. Similarly, references to Jesus are excluded in the passages of Scripture used in the ritual. For example, in the charge to the chapter in the Royal Arch, 2 Thessalonians 3:6-16 is read, omitting the name of Jesus as if the passage had nothing to do with Him. In the fourth degree, 1 Peter 2:5 is used, but with the reference to Jesus omitted. The same passages are used, mutilated in the same way, in Blue Lodge Masonry. (See chapter 10, "Masonry and the Bible.")

c. In the seventh (Royal Arch) degree, their blasphemous confession of the name of their god combines part of the sacred name of Yahweh (or Jehovah) with Baal or Bel, the pagan god ancient Israel was warned not to touch, and with On, representing Osiris, the Egyptian sun god (sex and fertility god), or Om, the generic Hindu name for their gods. In their most secret moment of ritual, they declare that the name of God is *YA-BEL-OM* or *JE-BUL-ON*. Spellings vary, but the supreme name of their god always combines the first sounds in Jehovah or Yahweh with Baal or Bel and On or Om (*Aum*).[1] Some Royal Arch Masons will deny that their name for their deity is a combination of Jehovah with Baal and On or Om, but Albert Pike, the quintessential Masonic authority, knew that that is precisely what it is. It is interesting that even Pike, patron saint of the Scottish Rite and author of the thoroughly pagan Masonic classic *Morals and Dogma*, was offended by what he called this "mongrel" name for deity.[2]

d. Worse, I believe, is their use of the name of God as a password in the Royal Arch chapters, taking this sacred name upon themselves and identifying *themselves* as the God of Abraham, Isaac, and Jacob. The challenge is, "Are you a Royal Arch Mason?" The reply is, "I am that I am."[3] This is horrible blasphemy!

e. The York Rite initiate must drink wine from a human skull, calling down a curse, the death of Judas (suicide), upon himself should he ever betray any of the secret work. In this same way, he also calls down upon himself the sins of the one from whose skull he drinks, in addition to his own. The Bible makes no provision for calling down curses upon ourselves and makes it clear that we are responsible for our own sins and no one else's.

f. As in the rest of Masonry, there is a horrible death oath for each degree of York Rite Masonry, in which the candidate agrees that, should he violate any of the secrecy or other provisions of the oath, he will allow himself to be mutilated and killed. For example, in the oath of the "Christian" Royal Arch, he swears to "no less a penalty than that of having my skull smote off, and my brains exposed to the scorching rays of the noonday Sun."[4] In the oath of the "Christian" degree of Knight Templar, he accepts "no less a penalty than that of having my head struck off and placed upon the highest spire in Christendom."[5]

g. Even if the York Rite were truly Christian and did not contain such awful blasphemies and occult, pagan ritual, it would still be true that the York Rite cannot divorce itself from the rest of Masonry. To be a member of the York Rite a man must continue to be a Blue Lodge Mason in good standing. "Veneration for, and fidelity to" Blue Lodge Masonry are declared in his York Rite initiation, and he must drink "libations" (drink offerings) to the "illustrious Grand Masters of Ancient Craft Masonry."[6] In addition, a York Rite Mason may also belong to the Scottish Rite, and it is not uncommon for the most dedicated (or ambitious) Masons to belong to both.

## 5. Does the history of the Order of Knights Templar (York Rite) go back to the Crusaders of the Middle Ages?

No, some writers claim this, but Knight Templarism in Masonry, like the rest of speculative Masonry, dates only from the eighteenth century. The Knight Templar degree was first conferred in America in 1769.

## 6. What were the medieval Knights Templar?

The medieval order of Knights Templar went to Palestine as crusaders in the early twelfth century to protect pilgrims and defend the temple site, where they made their initial headquarters. They were a combination religious and military order. Their last leader (early fourteenth century) was Jacques DeMolay. Their latter history is a murky and controversial one.

The Masonic version is that DeMolay and his templars were unselfish heroes, protecting and defending the Christian pilgrims journeying to Jerusalem, and that he was a martyr to the greed of the king of France and the pope (who also was French), both of whom feared his power and wanted his wealth.[7]

History records that the templars, who in the beginning took vows of poverty, diversified their activities and grew immensely wealthy, becoming in fact the most wealthy group in the world, with properties scattered throughout Christendom. They became "the great international financiers and bankers of the age with their Paris temple the center of the world's money market," in which "popes and kings deposited their revenues."[8] Their military might protected their widespread banks and bullion transfers. Sworn to absolute secrecy concerning their internal affairs, their secret, mysterious ritual meetings were held at midnight. Accused of corruption, witchcraft, and victimizing the pilgrims they were supposed to protect, they were greatly feared.

In 1305, evidence of their satanic corruption was obtained by means of a defector and spies sent by the king of France to infiltrate the order. On Friday, 13 October 1307, DeMolay and sixty templars were arrested in Paris.[9] DeMolay avoided torture and readily repented and tearfully confessed to "denying Christ and spitting on the cross." By joint order of the pope and the king of France, he and the rest were burned at the stake before Notre Dame as criminals and enemies of the faith, effectively ending the templars' power.[10] There is some evidence, however, that the enormous wealth of the templars has survived and evolved into the power base of the most powerful international banks of today.[11]

## 7. Then, what do the Masonic Knights Templar have to do with the medieval crusaders?

York Rite Masons take much of their symbolism from the medieval crusaders (defending the faith with their swords, etc.). Although they also claim to trace their actual history from Jacques DeMolay and the Crusades, the most credible Masonic authorities deny this. Albert Mackey, author of the *Encyclopedia of Freemasonry*, called the idea "wholly unsupported by the authority of history."[12] Albert Pike agrees that "they have assumed a title to which they have not a shadow of a claim."[13]

---

## Endnotes

1. Malcolm C. Duncan, *Duncan's Masonic Ritual and Monitor*, 3rd ed. (New York: David McKay Co., Inc., undated), 223-226.

2. Albert Pike, *The Holy Triad* (Washington, D.C., 1873).

3. Duncan, *Masonic Ritual*, 221.

4. Ibid., 230.

5. *In Hoc Signo Vincis*, 133, as quoted in Philip Lochaas, "American Rite Masonry" (Newtonville, NY: HRT Min, Inc., undated), 7-8.

6. Ibid., 139, 140.

7. This aspect of the story probably contains a certain amount of truth.

8. *Encyclopaedia Britannica*, vol. 21, 1957 ed., s.v. "Templars." There is an interesting theory to the effect that the templars found the hidden treasury of the temple, lost since Jerusalem was destroyed by Titus in A.D. 70, and that this was the beginning of their enormous wealth (for which there is no other known explanation).

9. This is believed by many to be the origin of the belief that Friday the thirteenth is an "unlucky" day.

10. The Order of DeMolay, the Masonic order for boys not yet old enough to join the Lodge, is named for this same Jacques DeMolay.

11. William T. Still, *New World Order* (Lafayette, LA: Huntington House, 1990), 112-114.

12. Albert Mackey, *Encyclopedia of Freemasonry*, rev. ed. s.v. "Templar" (Chicago, New York, London: Masonic History Co., 1927), 764.

13. Albert Pike, *Morals and Dogma*, rev. ed. (Washington, DC: House of the Temple, 1950), 821.

# 5

# The Shrine:
# Islam in Freemasonry

*Their sorrows shall be multiplied that hasten after another god: their drink offerings of blood will I not offer, nor take up their names unto my lips.*

—Psalms 16:4

## 1. Are the Shriners part of Masonry?

Yes, the Shrine (the full name is Ancient Arabic Order, Nobles of the Mystic Shrine) is the Islamic expression of Freemasonry. (See question 8, below.) It is one of the addendum groups within Masonry which has attracted wide interest and acceptance and become a major fixture within Freemasonry. The Shrine was first organized in New York in 1872.

## 2. Are these the men who wear the red hats with tassels and glittery decorations?

Yes, the Shrine is the most conspicuous part of Masonry; in fact, it is the only conspicuous part of Masonry. While the rest of Masonry is deliberately inconspicuous and maintains a low public profile, the Shrine is deliberately conspicuous and maintains a high public profile. They love to be in parades with their little motor scooters, go-carts, donkeys, or elephants and take clown acts to

hospitals and conduct circuses. People who know nothing
of the rest of Masonry will usually have some awareness of
the men in the red hats (fezzes), their circuses, all-star
football games, and hospitals for children.

### 3. How is the Shrine related to the rest of Masonry?

The Shrine's membership is restricted to those Masons who have advanced to the level of the Thirty-second
Degree or Knight Templar. After six months as either a
Thirty-second Degree Mason or Knight Templar, a man
may join the Shrine. This may sound like the Shrine is the
"top of the mountain" in Freemasonry, but it isn't; it is
actually an organization off to the side.

### 4. Does the rest of Masonry acknowledge the validity of the Shrine?

Absolutely. Although some of the purist students of
Masonry may look down upon it as a recent creation and
a less-than-pure form of Masonry, the vast majority of
Masons are proud of the Shrine. When anyone questions
the rightness of Masonry, the first thing a Mason will cite
to prove its goodness will be either George Washington
(See chapter 18, "Masonry, Presidents, and the Founding
Fathers.") or the good works of the Shriners.

### 5. What are the most common criticisms of the Shrine by other Masons?

There are no degrees in the Shrine, no lessons in
religion and morality. In fact, the position of being a
Shriner is not even a degree; he becomes a "Noble," but
this is not a degree. Also, the Shriners take a very light-
hearted approach to what they do, seeking "fun" in all
gatherings, and have earned a well-deserved reputation
for drinking a lot and conducting rowdy conventions. In
fact, for this reason some cities are reluctant to host their
conventions.[1] They are commonly referred to by other
Masons as "the party animals of Freemasonry." It is significant that the proper name for their local organization is
"club," in spite of the fact that their building is called

"temple." Their initiation ceremonies are particularly child-ish, rowdy, and often vulgar, featuring degrading, "bath-room" humor (see question 8, below). These initiations can be physically dangerous to the extent that a Shrine candidate must go through health screening prior to ini-tiation. In 1991, a Shriner sued his local Shrine club and six of its members for physical and emotional injury re-sulting from electric shock during his initiation.[2]

The Grand Lodge of England, where they take their Masonry very seriously, forbids its members to join such "fun" Masonic orders on penalty of dismissal.

## 6. What are their good works that offset all these criticisms?

The Shriners build and operate orthopedic hospitals and burn centers for children; the care is free for those who cannot pay. In 1993, there were twenty-three such hospitals in the United States, Canada, and Mexico.

## 7. So, how could there be anything wrong with a group that builds hospitals for children and provides free care?

The fact that a group does one thing that is good doesn't mean that everything else the group does is right.

## 8. Then, what about the Shrine is wrong?

What is wrong with the Shrine begins with the fact that it is part of the overall Masonic system. A man can't be a Shriner without being first, and continuously, a member in good standing of the Blue Lodge and either the Scottish Rite or the York Rite.

Additionally (and uniquely), the Shrine is the Islamic expression of Freemasonry, making it clearly anti-Chris-tian. Everything about the Shrine is based on the Muslim faith and Arabic symbolism. One soon notices that their costumes, symbols, and even the architecture and names of their temples are Arabic or Muslim.

The candidate for initiation is greeted by the high

priest, who says, "By the existence of Allah and the Creed of Mohammed, by the legendary sanctity of the Tabernacle at Mecca we greet you. . . ." The candidate must kneel before a Muslim altar, put his hand on the Koran (in some cases, also a Bible), and take his horrible death oath, calling upon the pagan god, Allah, for help: "May Allah, the god of the Arab, Moslim [sic] and Mohammedan, the god of our fathers, support me to the entire fulfillment of the same, Amen, Amen, Amen."[3]

In the recognition test ritual for a Shriner seeking to enter a Shrine meeting in a temple not his own, he is asked, among other things, at what Shrine he worships. He must answer, "At the Shrine of Islam."[4]

The Shrine ritual declares that Islam is truth: "Whoso seeketh Islam earnestly seeks true direction."[5] Since Islam and its holy book, the Koran, teach that Jesus was only a minor prophet, subordinate to Mohammed, that God has no sons, and that all "infidels" (and that includes us Christians) who will not renounce their faiths and convert to Islam are to be put to death, this creates a serious contradiction for the Christian Shriner.[6]

A minor and repulsive fact about the Shrine is its preoccupation with urination. In the roughhouse setting of the initiation, it appears to be merely bathroom humor, a matter of childish bad taste. The blindfolded candidate is sprayed with warm water and made to believe that he is being urinated upon by a dog or another man. Yet, in the serious matter of their "secret work," the recognition test by which a Shriner may be admitted to a lodge where he is not known refers to his having to "contribute a few drops of urine" in order to gain access to the meeting, reducing the Shriner to the cultural level of a dog.[7]

## 9. If the initiate must kneel before a Muslim altar and call upon Allah, the god of Mohammed, are there actually Christians who do this?

It seems impossible for a Christian to do such an obviously wrong and sinful thing, but they do. Pastors do.

With not only the obvious theological contradiction, but also the historic determination of the Muslims to eradicate the Jews and possess Palestine, it seems unthinkable that a Jew should also do this, but they do. Rabbis do.

In the case of most Shrine candidates, I believe that they don't take the Muslim matter or the oath seriously; they are just going through it all, getting it over with, so they can get on with the good works and the parties. But a pastor, priest, or rabbi who does such a thing must be one who is already terribly confused theologically, perhaps a universalist who thinks everyone will go to heaven (if there is such a place), that all gods are one, and that "all roads lead to the same mountaintop." They are wrong, and forever is a long time to be wrong.

## 10. But, what about the Shrine as a charity?

Here again, reality falls way short of the image they seek to project. Here also is an example of the kind of deception I have found throughout the Masonic system. In the first place, the impression that they seek to make is that every dime contributed to their hospital charities goes to help little children. That is certainly the belief of the person who gets stuck at the street intersection "roadblock" where he drops his money into the bucket marked "HELP CRIPPLED CHILDREN." Worse still, in a way, is that the Shriner standing there in the heat, cold, or rain, wearing his red fez and shaking the bucket at you with hope, also believes that every dime dropped in his bucket does go to help children. The reality is something quite different.

In 1986, the *Orlando Sentinel* published a landmark investigative series on the Florida Shrine and found that as little as 2 percent of the money collected in all of their fund-raising efforts actually went for building and operating their hospitals. The rest went to promotion, entertainment, publicity, operation of private bars, restaurants, and golf courses, travel, conventions (an estimated 15.5 million dollars spent on parties and conventions alone in

1986, according to the Internal Revenue Service), and accumulated wealth, which brings us to the second interesting point.

The Shrine is an extremely wealthy "charity." (To me, this seems to be a very great contradiction in terms.) In 1985, the IRS reported it as the wealthiest in the United States, with an estimated war chest of 2 billion dollars, approximately twice as wealthy as the one in second place, the American Red Cross, and four times as wealthy as the one in third place, the American Cancer Society. The Red Cross, however, spent four times as much in 1985 as the Shrine. In that year, according to the IRS, the Shrine spent only 29.8 percent of its income on program services, while the Red Cross spent 84 percent and the American Cancer Society spent 67.2 percent. In fact, no other charity in the top fourteen gave as little to designated assistance programs as the Shrine, the wealthiest of them all!

In 1985, according to IRS reports filed by the Shrine, they spent more money (15 million dollars) on parties and gala conventions than they did on their hospitals (12 million dollars). The same investigation (none of which was denied by the Shrine) disclosed that "Shrine hospitals get little support from Shrine Circuses, but most Shrine Temples could not pay their bills without an annual circus." An even more startling revelation of Shrine values was that "a Shriner may spend $180,000 to get elected to the Imperial Divan, the organization's national board of directors. Once elected, however, years of perks help make up for the cost."[8]

## 11. Does the Shrine require a death oath for membership?

Yes. Like the true degrees in Masonry, the Shrine also requires the candidate to take a death oath of obligation. In fact, this one is particularly gruesome, even when compared with the rest of Masonry's bloody oaths. In this oath, the candidate accepts the penalty of:

having my eyeballs pierced to the center with a three edged blade, with my feet flayed [sliced across in thin strips] and I be forced to walk the hot sands upon the sterile shores of the Red Sea until the flaming Sun shall strike me with livid plague.[9]

## 12. What is the significance of the red cap (the fez)?

The red cap is called a fez. It will usually have the name of the local Shrine club on the front in gold embroidery or sequins and is the essential item of dress for a Shriner. Some are extremely ornate (and expensive) and a matter of great personal pride. The red fez is the national headwear in Turkey, Egypt, and other Muslim countries. (It is interesting that in these countries, as in the Shrine, the fez may only be worn by men.)

The fez gets its name (and color) from the city of Fez in Morocco. Until the Muslim invaders overran it in the eighth century, Fez was a Christian city. When the city fell, the Muslim conquerors slaughtered thirty-five thousand Christians—men, women, and children—and their blood literally ran in the streets. The exultant Muslims celebrated their victory by dipping their wool caps in the Christians' blood and then wearing them in triumph. This is why it is called a fez, and this is why it is always red.

By wearing the red fez, Shriners are, in a sense, celebrating the slaughter of those Moroccan Christians. Most Shriners, of course, don't know this; if they did, most would laugh it off, saying, "We don't mean any such thing; we're just having fun," the classic Shriner justification for most of what they do.

## 13. But, don't some Masons excuse all this by saying that the Shrine isn't "official" Masonry?

Yes. When confronted with all this ugly truth, some knowledgeable Masons will try to explain it away by saying that the Shrine isn't really an "official" part of Masonry. For that matter, there is probably nothing in all the vast, complex system of Masonic orders and degrees that is "pure" Masonry except for the Blue Lodge, the first three degrees. But, if you go to the huge Masonic National Memorial, Masonry's national showpiece, towering just inside the beltway in Alexandria, Virginia, you will see a large portion of their space proudly devoted to the Ancient Arabic Order, Nobles of the Mystic Shrine.

No, the Shrine, where Allah is their god, Mohammed is their prophet, and fun is their principle occupation, is not only an inseparable part of American Freemasonry, it is probably the part of which Masons are most proud.

---

## Endnotes

1. In 1993, the question of whether or not to allow them to return was a hotly contested issue in New Orleans (certainly not an intolerant city), with many testimonies to irresponsible, destructive behavior by convening Shriners in the past.

2. Associated Press, *The Columbus Dispatch* (10 December 1991): 4-A.

3. *The Mystic Shrine, an Illustrated Ritual of the Ancient Arabic Order, Nobles of the Mystic Shrine,* rev. ed. (Chicago, IL: Ezra Cook Publishers, 1975), 18, 22.

4. *Shriners Recognition Test* (Chicago, IL: Ezra Cook Publishers, undated), 2.

5. Cook, *The Mystic Shrine*, 19.

6. The Koran, Surah 9:4, 5.

7. Cook, *Shriners Recognition Test*, 1.

8. John Wark and Gary Marx, "Shrine," *The Orlando Sentinel* (29 June 1986, A1; 30 June 1986, A1; 1 July 1986, A1).

9. Cook, *The Mystic Shrine*, 22.

# 6

## Adoptive Masonry: Masonic Groups for Women and Children

*Behold, there sat women weeping for Tammuz [Osiris]. Then He said to me . . . thou shalt see greater abominations than these. And He brought me into the Inner Court of the Lord's House, and behold . . . five and twenty men with their backs toward the Temple of the LORD, and their faces toward the east; and they worshipped the sun toward the east.*—Ezekiel 9:14-16

*The LORD God . . . will by no means clear the guilty; visiting the iniquity of the fathers upon the children. . . .*
—Exodus 34:6-7

### 1. Can women and children be Masons?

No. Membership in the Masonic Lodge is only for men. However, there are other groups related to the Masonic Lodge for women and children.

As a matter of interest, it is recorded that at least one woman has actually been initiated into the Masonic Lodge—by accident. This amazing event took place in Masonry's early days in Ireland. (See chapter 12, "Masonry's Exclusiveness and Elitism.")

## 2. What is the group for women?

Actually, there are several groups for women, including the Order of the Eastern Star, the Daughters of Isis, and the Daughters of the Nile. The Eastern Star is open to all women who are directly related to Master Masons in good standing (or to those who died in good standing). Some groups are more exclusive: the Daughters of Isis and the Daughters of the Nile are open only to the wives of Shriners, and the latter is by invitation only.

## 3. Are all these women's groups about the same?

No. While they are all basically the same in that they are Masonry-related—and this Masonic influence is apparent in their exclusiveness, secrecy, lofty titles, and pompous ceremony—the Eastern Star is relatively benign in its rituals, its oath is not bloody, much use is made of Scripture, and most of its members think it is Christian. The Daughters of Isis, on the other hand, is obviously pagan. The ritual is entirely based on the legend and worship of Isis and Osiris, its initiation is more like Blue Lodge Masonry, there is a horrible death oath, they must kiss the Koran and "the Red Stone of Horus," and not even the most deceived member would consider it "Christian."[1]

## 4. What is the Order of the Eastern Star?

The Order of the Eastern Star, open to all Mason-related women of age eighteen and above, is by far the largest women's group. The Star, as it is familiarly called, was the creation of Rob Morris, a prominent Kentucky Mason, poet, philosopher, and teacher, who wrote its degrees in 1850. Mississippi lays claim to being its birthplace, as the degrees were written and the first meeting was conducted by Morris in a rural Mississippi school building (which also served as the Masonic Lodge) while he was principal there. "The Little Red Schoolhouse" still stands and is preserved as an Eastern Star shrine in Holmes County, about ten miles south of Lexington, Mississippi, on State Route 17.[2] Today, the Eastern Star has grand chapters at state level, in U.S. territories, and several foreign countries, and a general grand chapter, with general authority, headquartered at the International Eastern Star Temple in Washington, D.C.

Women in the Eastern Star and the other groups "go through the chairs" (advance through the offices) just like their male sponsors in the Masonic Lodge.

## 5. Is the Eastern Star a Christian organization?

No, although most women who belong believe that it is. It can't be Christian, again like its male counterpart, for it is based upon and is a part of the overall Masonic Lodge system. Like the parent Blue Lodge of Masonry, their prayers are the Christless "universal" prayers of the rest of Masonry. Although there are references to Christ in the ritual, they are always indirect or inferred; the name of Jesus does not appear, even in their Eastern Star burial service.[3]

## 6. Why then do most of the members think "the Star" is a Christian organization?

Like most Blue Lodge Masons, members of the Eastern Star believe that it is a Christian organization because they were told this upon entering the order by sincere people who believed it to be true. Those who told them believed it because an earlier generation of sincere people told it to them, and so the deception is perpetuated from one generation to the next. With a strong belief in the Star as Christian and a right thing to do, they thenceforth blind themselves to a lot of contrary facts.

It is important to understand that they accept it because they are like most people who don't stop and think through what it means to be "Christian"—like us if we're not careful in how we apply our faith. If a Bible is involved, or Bible stories and characters included prominently in the rituals, and prayers (even if they are Christless prayers), most will call it "Christian." The exclusion of Jesus by name, secrecy, exclusiveness, references to the

Cabala, and other non-Christian characteristics go unnoticed by most.

Finally, their ritual statement, "We have seen his star in the East and are come to worship him," is assumed by practically all to refer to the Star of Bethlehem and the child, Jesus. It doesn't. As in the Masonic Lodge, the position of honor and worship is the east, not the west; the throne chairs of the Worthy Matron and Worthy Patron are against the east wall, under the symbol of deity. The Magi (wise men) of the Nativity of Jesus, however, came *from* the East. The star they saw and followed *was west of them*; they traveled from east to west and found the child Jesus in the west, not in the east.

Although few Eastern Star ladies realize it, east is their direction of honor and worship because the sun rises in the east. Since ancient times, pagan worshipers of nature and fertility have faced eastward and worshiped the reproductive, lifegiving power of the sun. Unwittingly, those nice ladies in their fine attire, with their candles and music, many of them well-meaning Christians, are reenacting this ancient pagan sex worship.[4] According to the most revered Masonic authorities, they are unwittingly participating in the worship of Isis and Osiris, which is phallic worship.[5] (See chapter 16, "Masonry and Symbolism," and chapter 20, "Masonry and the Occult.")

## 7. Can men belong to the Eastern Star?

Yes, most people don't realize this, but men can also belong to the Eastern Star if they are Master Masons in good standing. Although the Star is thought of as strictly a women's group, it was founded by men, the degrees and rituals were written by men, and a meeting can't even be conducted without the supervising presence of men. Each Eastern Star chapter has a male officer called "Worthy Patron" who oversees the functioning of the Worthy Matron (senior female leader). It is a violation of Eastern Star law to conduct any initiation without the Worthy Patron's presence, and such a thing may only be done under extraordinary circumstances with special permission.

## 8. What is the meaning of the pin, the five-pointed star emblem of the Eastern Star?

The five-pointed star is the basic emblem of the Order of the Eastern Star; it must be worn with the single point down. Each point is a different color and represents the virtues of the heroine of each of the five degrees of the order. The five-pointed star with the single point down is called a pentagram.

Although most members of the Eastern Star are unaware of it, there is a major theological and spiritual problem with their basic symbol. The five-pointed star with the single point down is the ancient and evil symbol of the Goat of Mendes, pagan god of lust, and, ultimately, Lucifer.[6]

Although Masonic historians are aware of this, it seems to be virtually unknown among the ladies of the Eastern Star. In fact, the pentagram is the most significant symbol in satanism; this symbol, stamped in gold on the cover of the white Eastern Star Bible, is likewise to be found on the cover of the Satanic Bible!

## 9. Is there a Masonic group for girls?

Yes. In fact, like the women, there are several Masonic orders for girls, including Job's Daughters and the Order of the Rainbow. The largest of these is the Order of the Rainbow, usually referred to as "Rainbow Girls." Rainbow Girls, affiliated with the Eastern Star, is for girls from age twelve to eighteen and is in a real way the "prep school" for the Eastern Star. The girls' orders have state and national structure, and the girls "go through the chairs" just like the women in the Eastern Star and their male sponsors in the Masonic Lodge. They even have their own (Christless) burial service!

## 10. And, what is there for boys?

For boys between the ages of fourteen and twenty-one there is the Order of DeMolay. As in the case of the Rainbow Girls, it can be thought of as the "prep school" for the Masonic Lodge. The boys in the Order of DeMolay wear black, scarlet-lined, "Dracula" type capes in their meetings, "go through the chairs," and have a national structure. The order is named for the famous (or infamous) Crusader, Jacques DeMolay, and its degrees are based on the Masonic version of his death. (See chapter 4, "Masonry's 'Christian' Degrees.")

## 11. Are these Masonic orders for women and children secret societies, or are their meetings open?

Like their parent organization, the Masonic Lodge system, they are secret societies. Their meetings are closed to the public, and they are sworn to secrecy concerning the ritual, key words, grips, signs, etc.

## 12. Can anyone of the right age join these groups?

Definitely not. Again, like their parent organization, the Masonic Lodge system, memberships in these "adoptive" orders are denied to certain groups and individuals. (See chapter 12, "Masonry's Exclusiveness and Elitism.")

## 13. What is the purpose of these groups?

In Masonic language, these Masonic orders for women and children are collectively called "adoptive Masonry." The name means just what it sounds like; these groups are "add-on" groups, not really part of Freemasonry as such, but externally attached, sponsored, and controlled by Masons. The idea of adoptive Masonry had its beginnings in France, where Masons wanted some way to include women in the Lodge. Rob Morris brought the idea to America and refined it. His stated purpose was to enable "worthy wives, widows, daughters and sisters of Freemasons" to be exposed to what he believed to be the beneficial influences of the Lodge and its teachings, without actually being initiated into its secrets.

## 14. What are their meetings like?

Like Masonic Lodge meetings, the meetings of the "adoptive" orders are extremely formal, wordy, pompous, and boring. Their titles are exalted, and the rituals complex. The lessons, lectures, and prayers are all "canned" and are recited from memory or read from script. They take themselves very seriously. Their ceremonies in costume or uniform can be lavish and colorful, and, in the women's and girls' groups, they can be beautiful, featuring pretty dresses, flowers, ribbons, candles, and pretty music.

Also, their meetings, initiations, and other rituals include the basic framework and much of the language of the parent Masonic Lodge. So much of the Masonic ritual and language has carried over into the groups for women and children that it has been a source of controversy among Masons, some fearing that their "secrecy" is thus partially compromised. If the women or children could go into a meeting of a Masonic Lodge, they would probably be amazed at the similarity, recognizing much of the ritual and language as their own and feeling right at home. Of course, in many ways they really would be, for their meetings are not only similar to those of the Masons but are often held in the very same room.

## 15. Is there a Masonic organization on college campuses?

Yes, "Acacia" is a social fraternity on many college and university campuses. It was organized at the University of Michigan in 1904 and was originally restricted to Masons on college campuses. Since 1933, however, its membership has been opened to include non-Mason males by invitation only. Its name is significant. Acacia is an important part of Masonic symbolism and ritual, representing redemption and everlasting life. The Acacia is an evergreen ("nondying") tree, common in Africa and the Middle East, similar in appearance to the American locust tree.

It figures significantly in the legend of Osiris in the Egyptian mystery religions.[7] (See also chapter 11, "Masonry and Religion.")

---

## Endnotes

1. National Imperial Court of the Daughters of Isis, "Ritual," (Chicago: Ezra Cook, undated): 1-16.

2. The name is misleading: "The Little Red Schoolhouse" is actually a fine, two-story brick building on a stone foundation, a veritable palace in light of its rural mid-nineteenth century surroundings.

3. General Grand Chapter, Order of the Eastern Star, *Ritual of the Order of the Eastern Star*, 22d ed. (Chicago, 1911), 119-133.

4. Albert Mackey, *Symbolism of Freemasonry* (Chicago: Chas. T. Powner Co., 1975), 333.

5. Ibid., 351,352; Albert Pike, *Morals and Dogma*, rev. ed. (Washington, DC: House of the Temple, 1950), 5, 757, 758, 771, 772.

6. Albert Mackey, *Encyclopedia of Freemasonry* (Masonic History Co.: Chicago, New York, London), rev. ed. s.v. "Pentagram," 1927, p. 553; L.C. Hascall, *History of the Ancient and Honorable Fraternity of Free and Accepted Masons*, and *Concordant Orders* (Boston and London: The Fraternity Publishing Co., 1891), 49, 101.

7. Mackey, *Symbolism of Freemasonry*, 313, 314.

# 7

# Masonry and Other
# Fraternal Orders

*For every tree is known by his own fruit.*

—Luke 7:44

## 1. Is Masonry connected with other fraternal orders like the Elks, Moose, Eagles, and Knights of Columbus?

No, at least they are not in any practical way. In terms of their origins, they can all be traced to the same pagan roots; but in terms of what they actually are today, with the exception of the Knights of Columbus, the others are very different from Masonry. The others have evolved to the place where they are primarily social, with very little emphasis on spiritual or moral matters. Initiation rites are similar but not taken nearly so seriously; likewise, matters of loyalty are not nearly as compelling.[1]

But, these things can't be said of the Knights of Columbus. The Order of the Knights of Columbus is so different from all the others as to need separate treatment. (See questions five through eight, below.)

## 2. Are these other groups as influential as the Masons?

No, not nearly. This is partly due to their "less serious" approach to themselves, but, in a practical way, it is primarily because of fewer numbers. In the same way that "success begets success," the opposite is true. As their numbers have dwindled, so has their attraction for new members. For the same reasons, the influential, prominent, and powerful are not attracted to these groups as they are to Masonry, a trend which perpetuates and magnifies itself.

## 3. Are they trying to reverse this trend?

They seem to be trying to capture some notice and gain credibility by taking on major public concerns. Of course, Masonry has stolen a gigantic march on them all with the Shriners' hospitals, but the others seem to be trying to find similar issues with which to identify. For example, the Elks clubs have taken up the battle against drugs.

## 4. Why do men join these other fraternal orders?

One reason men join the Elks, Moose, Eagles, Woodmen of the World, Odd Fellows, the Grange, and similar groups is for insurance purposes. Most of these fraternal orders, if not all, offer group insurance programs. A few initiates do seem interested in the spiritual aspect, however, and pursue that to some extent. Another major reason for joining these groups is social fulfillment. Such organizations usually maintain a clubhouse and carry on a busy program of social functions. In a dry county or district, where alcoholic beverages are prohibited, such a private club may be the only place where liquor may be bought and consumed, again a major attraction.

## 5. Are the Knights of Columbus part of the Masonic Lodge system?

Definitely not. Although there are some similarities, the Knights of Columbus is a separate system, in no way connected with Freemasonry.

## 6. In what way are the Knights of Columbus and Freemasonry similar?

The Order of Knights of Columbus is a closed fraternal order similar to Blue Lodge Masonry in that they have secret initiation rites, recognition signs, passwords, and grips. There is a commitment, as in all fraternal orders, to support and protect one another. The Order also has national organization, with local and regional authorities, published rituals, etc.

## 7. How then are the Knights of Columbus different from Masonry?

They are as different, almost, as night and day. Masonry is non-Christian (and as such, actually anti-Christian), nonsectarian, and universalist; Knights of Columbus is decidedly Christian in the sense that it is within the ecclesiastical system of the Roman Catholic church, it is under the authority of the Roman Catholic church, and one of its basic purposes is to promote the Catholic faith. Jesus is welcome in the Order of the Knights of Columbus. Because of the long-standing papal prohibition of Catholics from joining the Masonic Lodge, the Knights of Columbus and the Masonic Lodge are about as far apart in terms of doctrine as possible, in spite of superficial similarities.

Also, Knights of Columbus does offer an insurance program for its members, and Masonry never has.

## 8. Do the Knights of Columbus have to take bloody death oaths like the Masons do?

No, they do not, at least not for basic membership (three degrees). There is only one oath for all three degrees, and it is only one paragraph long. In the oath, the initiate promises to keep the secrets, to be loyal to the order and to the church, to be courteous to all, and to be true to God, the church, and to country. I find it interesting, however, that the oath is not taken in the name of

Jesus, nor in the name of the Triune God (Father, Son, and Holy Spirit).

The greatest threat to the initiate in the ritual is that he is reminded that the order is approved by and under the authority of the church so that to betray the order would be to betray the church, bringing a curse upon him (but not one for which he could not be forgiven). Otherwise the "secret work" (password, recognition signs, grips, etc.) is relatively simple and brief.[2]

## Endnotes

1. *Secret Societies Illustrated* (Chicago, IL: Ezra Cook Publications, undated), 59-99.

2. Thomas C. Knight, *Knights of Columbus, Illustrated* (Chicago, IL: Ezra Cook Publications, 1974), 89-93.

# 8

## Masonry's Membership: Why Men Join

*There is a way that seemeth right unto a man, but the end thereof are the ways of death.*

—Proverbs 16:25

### 1. Why do men join the Masonic Lodge?

Men join the Masonic Lodge for a variety of reasons. Some join because of the mystique; it appeals to them to belong to something exclusive and "secretive." A very few will join for spiritual reasons, seeking occult knowledge; some are simply looking for God and don't know where to find Him. Many join because of peer pressure. But, by far, the most common reason for joining is to gain social, political, and business advantage.

### 2. Do Masons actually join for personal gain?

Definitely. Most candidates have been told, or have simply observed, that "things go better" for those who are Masons. Although, theoretically, men are not supposed to join for such self-serving reasons, any honest Mason will admit that this is the most common motivation. Prior to being initiated into the first degree, the candidate is asked if he is joining for any self-serving reason. Most have been told about this question in advance by their friends in the

Lodge and are told to answer, "No." It is interesting to me that this is the only part of the initiation about which the candidate is told in advance, and this single exception is made so that he can be prompted to lie.

## 3. Is there real advantage in being a Mason?

Absolutely. It is true that Masons give preferential treatment to other Masons. If two men are competing for the same contract, appointment, scholarship, promotion, etc., and one is a Mason, the other isn't, and the one who makes the decision is also a Mason, the Masonic candidate will probably be selected. If the setting is a civil or criminal court, the consequences can be much more serious. (See chapter 17, "Death Oaths and Masonic Execution.")

## 4. Does Masonry run in some families?

Yes. A very common and powerful motivation for joining the Lodge, especially in the South, is family tradition. When a man's father, uncles, and grandfathers have been Masons, there is great pressure to conform to the family tradition and enter the Lodge. Whether he is really interested or not, joining is often something assumed, and most such young men wouldn't even consider not joining. A young man might not really want to be a Mason but will join anyway, for to fail to join would be an affront, or at least a disappointment, to his relatives and a denial of his ancestry. I really believe that this is why my father did it. He entered the Lodge as a very young man, apparently to please the older men in the family, and then he later left it behind.

## 5. Do some join for the social life?

Yes, and the social life, the human fellowship, is real. There is very close human fellowship in the Lodge, a kind of social bonding that comes from shared experience and commitment. It is also no secret that there is an ongoing round of carry-in dinners, parties, and other social functions associated with the Lodge, not just for the Mason, but also for his family. A man becomes part of it all when he joins (and, incidentally, he immediately loses it all if he should leave the Lodge).

## 6. Do some men join because they have to?

Yes, it is that simple in some cases. In some settings and industries, a man will not be hired if he is not a Mason. One man, now a pastor, told me that as a young man he was forced to join the Lodge in order to be hired by a railroad and said that to his knowledge this requirement was universal at the time throughout the railroad industry.

## 7. Is there ever pressure on ministers to join the Lodge?

Yes. It occurs especially in some denominational groups. Although some denominations forbid their ministers and priests to join the Masonic Lodge, in others there is a considerable pressure to join. Young Baptist ministers are often told by the older ones that if they want to "succeed," they should join the Lodge. The same is true, if not more so, among United Methodist ministers, where Masonry is well entrenched.

## 8. What about the armed forces?

There is pressure to join the Lodge in the armed forces; in fact, "Sojourners" is a Masonic group just for members of the armed forces, in effect a traveling lodge. In my experience, this pressure manifests itself most often in the air force and the army and is more common in the upper enlisted ranks, where it can have an impact on promotion, especially in the very highest grades. Interestingly, in all my years as a marine, enlisted and commissioned, I never saw any sign of Masonry's presence or influence in the Marine Corps.

# 9

# Masonry's Membership: How Men Join

*An inheritance may be gotten hastily at the beginning; but the end thereof shall not be blessed.*

—Proverbs 20:21

## 1. How does a man enter the Masonic Lodge?

In theory, the candidate must enquire. He must somehow notice the existence of Masonry—the ring, guarded conversations from which he is excluded, the exchange of coded expressions and knowing looks, etc.—then ask about Masonry and how he may join.

This is the theory. Theory and reality are sometimes very different.

## 2. Do the Masons ever recruit new members?

In theory, Masonry doesn't recruit; one must ask to be a Mason, for he will not be invited to join. You may see bumper stickers that say, somewhat cryptically, "2 B 1 ASK 1." If you see such a bumper sticker, it will be on a Mason's car, and this bumper sticker is a typical Masonic contradiction. The expanded translation of the coded message is "To be one of us, you must ask one of us." Since this invites the curious to ask what it means and then ask about joining, it is a recruiting device, doing exactly what it says must not be done.

## 3. But, do they really recruit—actually go after new members?

Yes, at times, they do just that. The recruiting approach can be very subtle, very aggressive, or something in between. Masons can subtly engage in suggestive conversation around a prospect, conversation designed to inspire curiosity so that he will ask about the Lodge. A very common occurrence, and a step beyond this approach, is for a Mason simply to say to a prospect that Masonry is a fine institution and ask if he isn't interested in finding out about it. It is not uncommon for a Mason to say to a friend something like, "The Lodge is a fine organization, it has been good for me, and you would be wise to look into it."

Sometimes, as we have already seen in chapter 8, recruiting becomes outright coercion. A man is given to understand, one way or another, that if he wants to "get ahead" (or even be hired), he must join the Masonic Lodge.

In recent years, with more and more unflattering truth being made public about Masonry, they have taken to billboard advertisements. Some have a photo of a prominent person and his testimony as to the benefits Masonry has brought into his life; others simply state the claims of the institution ("Masonry builds character in men.") or trumpet the good works (e.g., Shrine hospitals, Masonic retirement homes, orphanages, etc.).

It is unusual, but there have even been times when a temporary Masonic lodge room was set up in a semi-trailer in a busy shopping center parking lot and men initiated right there on the spot.

## 4. Once a man expresses interest or willingness to join the Lodge, what happens next?

After the inquirer expresses interest in Masonry, or a willingness to join, he is told a little about the group, enough to get him started. He must find two Masons willing to sponsor him and recommend him in writing to the local lodge.[1] Within a few days, he will be visited by an investigating committee; the purpose of the visit is to ascertain whether or not the candidate is "good enough" to become a Mason.[2] If the man is acceptable, he is subsequently contacted and told when to report to the lodge hall for initiation.

## 5. If the visiting committee finds the candidate acceptable, is he automatically taken into the Lodge?

No. A ballot of the Lodge membership is taken. Balloting is strictly secret and is done by means of dropping a small ball into a ballot box. A white ball is a "yes" vote, and a black ball is a "no" vote. To be taken into the Lodge, the "yes" vote must be unanimous. If all the balls are white, the ballot is said to be "clear," and the man is accepted. If there is even one black ball, the candidate is rejected. In Masonic language, that man has been "blackballed."

## 6. What does it cost to become a Mason?

Costs vary from state to state (grand lodge to grand lodge) and even from local lodge to local lodge within a state (grand lodge); but, regardless of the variation, there will always be an initiation fee for each degree. It is common to pay for all three degrees of the Blue Lodge at once, before being initiated into the first degree. If a man goes on into the higher degrees of the York Rite or the Scottish Rite, there are additional initiation fees for those degrees (usually paid for in degree "clumps" in the higher degrees). If he then goes into the Shrine, there is still another fee for that. The same is true of the Order of the Eastern Star, Tall Cedars of Lebanon, Jesters, or other appendant groups, should a Mason join them. In addition to the initiation fees, there are annual dues for each affiliation (separate dues for the Blue Lodge, the York Rite, the Scottish Rite, the Eastern Star, etc.).

The total cost for one who goes on into the higher degrees can run into the thousands of dollars, and the initiation fees must be paid for each order, degree, or group of degrees before initiation begins. In addition to the initiation fees, there are the annual dues, which the man is to go on paying for life.

## 7. Are there any tests or examinations to pass in order to join?

Yes, in the Blue Lodge there are. There is considerable memory work to be done in the Blue degrees, and a member of the Lodge is appointed to be the instructor for each incoming group of initiates. (Ordinarily, two or more men will be initiated together.) This instructor meets with the candidates on appointed nights in the lodge hall and helps them memorize the "secret work" of the degree into which they have just been initiated. This is very much like the way candidates for confirmation in a liturgical church are taught the catechism in preparation for examination and confirmation by the bishop. When the candidates are ready, they must recite acceptably before the assembled members of the lodge in order to be initiated into the next degree.

## 8. What is it that they must learn?

They must learn the Masonic catechism. For example, they are asked, "What makes you a Mason?" The correct answer is "My obligation." In addition to this, they must memorize the "secret work" of the degree, such as the grip, penalty sign, dueguard password, etc. The most difficult learning challenge is the oath of obligation, which they must memorize word for word (after, it must be pointed out, the oath has been taken; the candidate is never told of the oath before he is told to repeat it, a few words at a time, after the Worshipful Master).

## 9. Must they do all this memorizing for the higher degrees?

No. Although there is a death oath of obligation, grip, and password for each higher degree, they are demonstrated only and there is no memorization to do once the oath is taken. Blue Lodge Masons who don't know this imagine the awesome work involved in becoming a Thirty-second Degree Mason because they know how much they had to work to memorize all that stuff for the three degrees. Receiving the higher degrees is mostly a matter of sitting in a theater, watching as the degree is presented in a drama ("exemplified") or merely listening to it as a lecture ("communicated"), and then taking the oath. Higher degree Masons seldom remember the oaths they have taken because they take so many in a short time and they do not have to memorize them.

## 10. How long does it take to go through all this and get the degrees?

In the Blue Lodge, the time required varies depending on how long it takes the incoming initiates to learn the material. A man could go through all three of the Blue degrees in as little as a few weeks or as long as a few months. Perhaps five or six weeks would be the average time for the entire process in the Blue Lodge.

In the higher degrees, a group initiation is done in one weekend. In the Scottish Rite, this is normally done in two successive weekends, with the fourth through the fourteenth degrees taken the first weekend and the fifteenth through the Thirty-second degrees taken in the second weekend. This occurs twice a year, normally fall and spring, and they call these convocations "reunions." In the York Rite, the process is essentially the same, with the degrees organized into three groups: Capitular Rite, Cryptic Rite, and Chivalric Rite.

## 11. Is a man given his Masonic ring when he is taken into the Lodge?

No. With the exception of the Scottish Rite, rings are not presented, they are selected and purchased privately. All those Masonic rings one sees, with a colored stone embossed in gold with the Masonic emblem, are purchased by the individual Mason. That's why there are so many variations in color and style; manufacturers simply make them and distributors market them, and anyone can buy one, as is the case with lapel pins and other Masonic jewelry. It is not even necessary to be a Mason in order to buy such things since Masonic rings and other jewelry can be bought through catalogs. The same is true of the jewelry for the Eastern Star and other "adoptive" Masonic groups. There is no such thing, outside the Scottish Rite, as an "official" Masonic ring.

In the Scottish Rite, the Thirty-second Degree ring is normally presented with the Fourteenth Degree at the end of the first reunion weekend. (You probably think this is a typographical error, but it isn't; they really do present the Thirty-second Degree ring with the Fourteenth Degree, strange as it seems, and some Masons call it the Fourteenth Degree ring.) This ring is a plain, flat, gold band exactly like a plain gold wedding ring except that it has a small triangle with the Hebrew letter *yod* stamped in it. There is a second such ring, given with the Thirty-third Degree, and it looks just the same except that it has "33" inside the triangle.

It is interesting to me that the only real Masonic ring would never be recognized as such without some insider knowledge of Masonry (which, of course, you now possess).

## 12. Is it true that a married man must remove his wedding ring in order to be initiated into the Masonic Lodge?

Yes, and most wives would be offended if they knew this. The initiate must remove all his rings and other jewelry, along with his clothes, in order to be initiated into the Blue Lodge.

## 13. Do you mean that Masons must take off their clothes to be initiated?

Yes. This is to make the point that the initiate brings nothing to the process of initiation; rather, he is poor, naked, helpless, has nothing "going for him," and is totally dependent on the Worshipful Master and the Lodge to redeem him and bring him out of his present wretched condition.

## 14. Does he go through the initiation naked?

No, it is more like he is half-naked. In the preparation room, after he takes his own clothes off, he is given a simple cotton shirt and trousers, much like pajamas, and he is told to put them on. In each of the first two degrees, he has one or the other leg rolled up high and the shirt half off his torso; in the third degree, he has both legs rolled up high and the shirt completely off. In all three degrees, he is completely blindfolded and is led (i.e., jerked, dragged) around the room by a rope called a "cabletow." In the first degree (the most frightening), the rope is tied around his neck. In the second degree, it is around his shoulder. In the third degree, it is tied around his waist.[3]

## 15. Why is he blindfolded?

This is probably the most important aspect of the initiation, especially for a Christian. The blindfold makes the point that the candidate is in complete spiritual darkness and needs the Worshipful Master and the Lodge to bring him out of spiritual darkness and into the light of redemption. For a Christian to do this is a blasphemous denial of his true Redeemer and an outright denial of Scripture such as John 8:12, "I am the light of the world; he that followeth me shall not walk in darkness, but shall have the light of life."

Incidentally, the proper Masonic term for the blindfold is "hoodwink," and an initiate so blindfolded is said in Masonic terminology to be "hoodwinked."

## 16. Is there really a rope tied around his neck?

Absolutely, in the first degree. In the second and third degrees, it is tied around the shoulder and the waist, respectively, as we have already noted. In many lodges, this rope, called a "cabletow," is blue.

## 17. But, what is its purpose?

With this rope, the hoodwinked candidate is led around the room during the ritual of initiation like a blind dog on a leash.

## 18. But, what is the purpose of all this? Why is the man treated this way?

The effect, and its apparent purpose, is humiliation. The candidate is "reduced to nothing" in this way; he is poor, blind, naked, helpless, confused, and afraid. In addition, he has no idea of where he is, who is watching him, or how many there are. It is a powerful means of subjugation and mind control and may have a permanent detrimental effect on the man, binding him mentally and spiritually to the Lodge and its authority.

## 19. Does the candidate know in advance what his initiation will be like?

Definitely not. This seems to be part of its impact, at least in the first degree. There is, naturally, less surprise in the second and third degrees, having already experienced the first degree.

## 20. Does the candidate know about the death oath in advance?

No, at least he does not in the first degree. He doesn't even know that there will be an oath, let alone the horrible, bloody nature of it. He may suspect such oaths in the second and third degrees, after experiencing the first, but he is definitely never told in advance.

In this way, the Ku Klux Klan is more honorable and straightforward than the Masonic Lodge. In the Klan, a candidate not only knows in advance that there will be an oath, he is required to read it in advance so that he will know, exactly, that to which he is going to swear. And, the oath of the Klan is not even a bloody death oath as is the one in the Lodge. In the Lodge, he not only doesn't know the nature of the oath in advance, he doesn't even know there is going to be one. Disoriented, blindfolded, half naked, and with a rope around his neck, he is told to kneel and place his hand on the Bible (or other "holy book"). Then, an authoritative voice in front of him (It is the Worshipful Master, but he doesn't know that.) says, "Repeat after me . . . ," and the candidate repeats the oath, a few words at a time.[4]

## 21. Does the candidate, once he learns what the initiation is really like, ever just get up and leave?

Almost never. Once the process is begun, the emotional and spiritual pressures to continue are very great. Even a Christian, under immediate conviction that what he is doing is wrong, will almost always go through with it. He knows that all the Masons whom he knows, perhaps including his father, grandfather, deacons, elders, or pastor of his church, went through with it, so he thinks that it must be alright, although his mind and the Holy Spirit are telling him that it is wrong.

## 22. Can a man become a Mason without going through initiations?

Yes. Becoming a Mason without being initiated is called being made a Mason "at sight." This is ordinarily done only for very important people, such as high-ranking political figures, heads of state, celebrities, etc. The process can vary from jurisdiction to jurisdiction but usually consists of a Grand Master (or other man of equal or higher position) going to the office of the honoree (or some other suitable location), reading the ritual, and declaring the individual to be a Mason.[5]

## Endnotes

1. It is interesting that this recommendation is called "a recommend" (using a verb as if it were a noun), the same odd name given in Mormonism to the document needed to enter the temple. There is an intimate relationship between Masonry and Mormonism. (See chapter 21, "Masonry and Mormonism.")

2. The candidate is almost always found to be acceptable; there must be something very wrong with a man in order for him to be rejected.

3. Malcolm C. Duncan, *Duncan's Masonic Ritual and Monitor,* 3rd ed. (New York: David McKay Co., undated), 7-96.

4. Ibid.

5. George W. Chase, *Digest of Masonic Law,* 8th ed. (Boston: Pollard and Leighton, 1869), 60-65.

# 10

# Masonry and the Bible

*Every word of God is pure . . . add thou not unto His words.*
—Proverbs 30:5

## 1. Is Masonry based upon the Bible?

No. One of the most common misconceptions about Freemasonry, especially among Masons, is that it is based on the Bible. Nothing could be further from the truth.

## 2. Do Masons believe that Masonry is based on the Bible?

Yes, with few exceptions, they certainly do. One of the first things most Masons will say to defend the "rightness" of belonging to the Masonic Lodge is that it can't be wrong, for it is based on the Bible. Among the rank and file, where one is most likely to hear this assertion, they believe this.

## 3. If Masonry isn't based on the Bible, why do most Masons believe it is?

Most Masons, especially in the "Bible Belt," are told at the outset that Masonry is based on the Bible. Virtually all of them believe this, and go on believing this, in spite of the fact that so much of what they see and hear for the rest of their Masonic lives indicates that it isn't. Except for a few serious students of Masonry, they go on believing this because the Bible is always on the altar, because some verses of Scripture are used in the ritual, and because Bible characters and events are used in some of the degrees. There is even a Masonic Bible, usually presented to the newly made Master Mason, and this strengthens the deception.

## 4. If there is a Bible open on the altar, why do you say that Masonry is not based on the Bible?

The fact that the Bible is on the altar in the Masonic Lodge no more proves that the Lodge is based on it than a Bible on a coffee table means that the family is Christian and living according to the Bible. Even if it did, then how do we explain all those lodges where they have the Koran, the Hindu Vedas, or some other "holy book" on the altar in place of the Bible?[1] Even in those lodges where there is an open Bible on the altar, there are also the Masonic square and compass, lying on top of it, in the superior position.

## 5. What then is the official status of the Bible in the Masonic Lodge?

Masonic literature refers to the Bible as a part of the "furniture" of the lodge. In lodges where the Bible is used, candidates put their hands on the Bible to take their oaths of obligation and then are required to kiss it.

In the Blue Lodge (the first three degrees), candidates are taught that the Bible is "the rule and guide for faith and practice" (some say, "*a* rule and guide") and that it is one of the three "Great Lights of Masonry."[2]

## 6. If they say that the Bible is their rule and guide for faith and practice and their great light, doesn't that mean that Masonry is based on the Bible?

No, in fact this is one of the many contradictions in Masonic doctrine. They say that the Bible is "the rule and guide for faith and practice" yet reject or ignore much of its clear teachings, especially those concerning Jesus, redemption, and its claims about itself.[3]

The Bible is very clear in saying that there is only one true and living God, only one Mediator between God and men (the man, Christ Jesus), that every part of the Bible is inspired ("God-breathed"), and that no one is to take away from or add to it. Yet, Masonry honors pagan gods, reduces Jehovah to the level of Buddha or Krishna, and worships a generic god called the Great Architect of the Universe. Masonry denies the divinity and uniqueness of Jesus as Savior, reducing Him to the status of just one of the great men of the past. And, Masonry feels free to alter Scripture by removing references to Jesus from all New Testament verses used in the ritual, as if those verses had nothing to do with Him, even though the Bible clearly forbids this.[4]

Herein is a most significant and revealing thing about Masonry, expressing clearly the true attitude of the Masonic philosophers toward both Jesus and the Bible. The removal of references to Jesus from verses of the New Testament used in the ritual is an eloquent expression of Masonry's contempt for both Jesus and the Bible. An example is the verse used in the charge to a regular meeting of the Blue Lodge, 2 Thessalonians 3:6: "Now we command you brethren, in the name of our Lord Jesus Christ, that ye withdraw yourselves from every brother that walketh disorderly, and not after the tradition that ye received from us." In the Lodge ritual, the words "in the name of our Lord Jesus Christ" are arbitrarily removed from the verse, as if it had nothing to do with Him. This butchering out of such references to Jesus from the Bible (and this is not the only one) is a blasphemous insult both to Him and to the Word of God, a direct violation of the Bible's teachings about itself. Albert Mackey, revered Masonic authority, calls such mutilations of Scripture "slight, but necessary, Modifications."[5]

Yet, this same Albert Mackey, in his authoritative work, *Jurisprudence of Freemasonry*, says that the Masonic writings are perfect and must not be changed in any way! Let's hear him in his own words: "The Landmarks (fundamental doctrines) of Masonry are so perfect that they neither need nor will permit of the slightest amendment."[6]

A related and revealing fact is that while the Bible is the unique, unchanging, inspired Word of God to the Christian, in Masonry the Bible is only one of their "three great lights." The square and compass are the other two, and remember where they are: on top of the Bible, in the superior position, on the Masonic altar. And, that's not all. In lodges where the Koran or Hindu Vedas is on the altar in place of the Bible, the square and compass must always be there. The square and compass are clearly more important in Masonry than the Bible.

Do you still need convincing? Let's hear again from Albert Mackey:

> An attempt has been made by some Grand Lodges to add to these simple, moral and religious qualifications, another, which requires a belief in the divine authenticity of the Scriptures. It is much to be regretted . . . .[7]

So, for Masonry to say that the Bible is the (or even *a*) rule and guide for faith and practice and then to ignore and violate its most important teachings, is an obvious and outrageous contradiction. No, in no way is Masonry "based on the Bible."

## 7. Do any of the leading Masonic authorities say that Masonry is based on the Bible?

No, in fact, they say just the opposite. I will quote only four, but there are many more.

> The place of the Bible in Freemasonry is as difficult to fix as are some of the [religious] beliefs adverted [sic] to above.[8]

> The Bible is an indispensable part of the furniture of a Christian lodge only because it is the sacred book of the Christian religion. The Hebrew

Pentateuch in a Hebrew lodge, and the Koran in the Mohammedan one, belong on the altar; and [any] one of these, and the Square and Compass, properly understood, are the Great Lights by which a Mason must walk.[9]

Thus the Trestleboard [blueprint for life] of the Jews is the Old Testament, of the Mohammedan, the Koran; the Vedas Scriptures of Hinduism and the writings of Baha-ullah are just as good as the Word of the Christians' God, for the fact is that all religions are never as good as the pure teachings of Freemasonry.[10]

The Jews, the Chinese, the Turks, each reject either the New Testament, the Old, or both, and yet we see no good reason why they should not be made Masons. In fact, Blue Lodge Masonry has nothing whatever to do with the Bible. It is not founded on the Bible; if it was it would not be Masonry, it would be something else.[11]

## 8. What is the Masonic Bible?

The Masonic Bible is merely the King James Bible with the basic Masonic symbol on the cover and a section of Masonic teachings in the front. One of the most interesting things about the Masonic Bible is that the Masonic teachings in the front of their Bible are in direct contradiction with the Bible itself. Two examples of this are the "Masonic Creed" and the section on "The Great Light in Masonry." Let me explain:

*The Masonic Creed.* This is their statement of basic beliefs and, right there at the beginning of their Bible, presents another glaring contradiction in Masonry. Of these six statements of fundamental Masonic belief, three are in conflict with the Bible itself, and another is simply untrue:

(1) "There is one God, the Father of all men." But, the Bible says that God is the creator of all men, but is no one's father until redeemed by faith in Christ Jesus.

(2) "Character determines destiny." In simple words, this means that "good" people go to heaven, "bad" people go to hell, and we must save ourselves by being "good." Jesus is unnecessary in this plan of salvation. (See chapter 13, "Masonry and Jesus Christ.")

(3) "Prayer, communion of man with God, is helpful." Helpful? This anemic statement is in fact a subtle lie; the Bible doesn't say that prayer is "helpful," the Bible says that prayer is essential and commands it!

(4) The statement that is simply untrue is that the Bible is the great light in Masonry and the rule and guide for faith and practice. (See question 6, above.)

***The Great Light in Masonry.*** This belief statement on the Bible is written by the revered Masonic authority, the Reverend Dr. Joseph Fort Newton. The pertinent passages are too extensive to quote here, but he states that the Bible is merely "a symbol" of the will of God, a part of man's ever-changing understanding of God, that it teaches us to revere the "book of faith" of the Muslim and Hindu, and that the Christian and all the pagan religions worship the same "Nameless one of a hundred names," praying to the same "God and Father of us all." He says that "Masonry knows, what so many forget, that religions are many, but Religion is one." (In other words, all religions are actually the same and of equal value.) He then goes on to agree with the poet Lowell, that the true Bible is not a book written on paper, but is the ongoing accumulation of human experience and wisdom.

As is the case with Jesus, here is a very serious problem: a watered-down Bible is no Bible at all.

## 9. If Masonry is not based on the Bible, then on what is it based?

Masonry is based on the Cabala (variously spelled as Kaballa, Quaballah, etc.). I could fill this book with authentication on just this one subject. That, of course, would be impractical; let's allow two of Masonry's most honored writers of doctrine to speak briefly on this subject:

Albert Pike, the preeminent writer of Masonic doctrine, made clear the position of the Cabala:

> Masonry is a search after light. That search leads us back, as you see, to the Kaballah.[12]

> All truly dogmatic religions have issued from the Kaballah, and return to it; everything scientific and grand in the religious dreams of the Illuminati, Jacob Boeheme, Swedenborg, St. Martin and others, is borrowed from the Kaballah; all Masonic associations owe to it their secrets and their symbols.[13]

J.D. Buck, most highly esteemed contemporary Masonic philosopher, concurs:

> The Kabalah alone consecrates the alliance of the Universal Reason and Divine Word; it establishes . . . the eternal balance of being; it alone reconciles Reason with Faith, Power with Liberty, Science with Mystery; it has the keys to the Present, the Past and the Future. The Bible, with all the allegories it contains, expresses, in an incomplete and veiled manner only, the religious science of the Hebrews.[14]

Again, Buck explains:

> Drop the theological barnacles from the Religion of Jesus, as taught by Him, and by the Essenes and Gnostics of the first centuries, and it becomes Masonry. Masonry in its purity, derived as it is from the old Hebrew Kabalah . . .[15]

Even in the doctrine of the relatively benign Order of the Eastern Star, their code word is called their "Cabbalistic [based on the Cabala] Word."[16, 17]

## 10. If Masonry is based on something called "the Cabala," what is the Cabala?

The Cabala (variously spelled) is a medieval Jewish book of occult philosophy and magic based on mystical interpretations of the Old Testament.[18] It is sometimes published in more than one volume and sometimes in applicable portions. "Cabalistic" (also variously spelled) is the adjective form denoting anything derived from the Cabala. The Cabala is popular with, and important to, magicians, sorcerers, witches, and satanists, as well as Masonic philosophers. It is, interestingly, also very important to Hasidic Jews. The Hasidim are thought of as the most strictly fundamentalist Jews; yet, in their use of "scriptures," they are far from the Word of God delivered to Moses and the Prophets.

## 11. Then, what does Masonry really teach about the Bible?

There are three themes that are consistent in what the most respected Masonic philosophers write; in very brief form, they are as follows:

• The Bible is merely one of the "holy books" of the world's religions, no better or worse than the Koran, the Hindu scriptures, the Book of Mormon, or the Tibetan Book of the Dead. (See questions 7 and 8, above.)

• The Bible is not the final, complete revelation of the will and Word of God. Rather, they teach that the Bible is incomplete, distorted, and merely "a symbol" of both. The real Bible, they teach, is the ongoing accumulation of human knowledge of the nature and will of God. (See question 8, above, The Great Light in Masonry.)

• The obvious meaning of the Bible, that is, what it actually says, is not true. As in all doctrinal matters, Masonic writers recognize two meanings of all teachings: the outer, obvious meaning, and the inner, hidden meaning. Because of their love for impressive language, they call the outer, obvious meaning the *exoteric* meaning. The inner, hidden meaning they call the *esoteric* meaning.

The hidden meaning, the esoteric meaning, is always the true one, and the obvious meaning, the exoteric meaning, is untrue and only for the ignorant, unthinking masses. Albert Pike, that preeminent Masonic authority, wrote much on this, including the following about the Bible:

> What is truth to the philosopher, would not be truth, nor have the effect of truth, to the peasant. The religion of many [the ordinary people] must necessarily be more incorrect than that of the refined and reflective few. . . . The doctrines of the Bible are often not clothed in the language of strict truth, but in that which was fittest to convey to a rude and ignorant people . . . the doctrine.[19] . . . The literal meaning [of the Bible] is for the vulgar only.[20]

## Endnotes

1. In Muslim lodges, Hindu lodges, and the lodges of other non-Judeo-Christian faiths, there will be on the altar their "holy book" in place of the Bible; in a Jewish lodge, there will be the Old Testament only.

2. According to Masonic doctrine, the "Three Great Lights of Masonry" are the Square, the Compass, and the Bible. The "Three Lesser Lights of Masonry" are the Sun, the Moon, and the Worshipful Master of the Lodge.

3. Deuteronomy 4:35, 32:39; 1 Timothy 2:5; John 14:6; Acts 4:12; Psalms 12:6,7; 2 Timothy 3:16; Revelations 22:18,19; et al.

4. Ibid.

5. Albert Mackey, *The Masonic Ritualist* (New York: MaCoy Publishing Co., 1903), 272.

6. Albert Mackey, *Jurisprudence of Freemasonry*, rev. and enlarged ed. Book II (Chicago: Chas T. Powner Co., 1975), 57.

7. Ibid.

8. Henry W. Coil, *Masonic Encyclopedia*, s.v. "Religion" (New York: MaCoy Publishing Co., 1961), 518.

9. Albert Pike, *Morals and Dogma*, rev. ed. (Washington, DC: House of the Temple, 1950), 11.

10. Mackey, *The Masonic Ritualist*, 59.

11. George W. Chase, *Digest of Masonic Law*, 8th ed. (Boston: Pollard and Leighton, 1869), 207, 208.

12. Pike, *Morals and Dogma*, 741.

13. Ibid., 744.

14. J.D. Buck, *Mystic Masonry*, 3rd ed. (Chicago: Chas T. Powner Co., 1925), 42.

15. Ibid., 66.

16. Their secret "Cabbalistic word" is *Fatal*, meaning "Fairest among thousands, altogether lovely."

17. Robert MaCoy, *Adoptive Rite Ritual* (New York: MaCoy Publishing and Masonic Supply Co., 1942), 87; *Order of the Eastern Star Recognition Test* (Chicago, IL: Ezra Cook Publications, 1975), 2, 3.

18. Cabala or Cabbala: "An occult theosophy of rabbinical origin, widely transmitted in medieval Europe, based on an esoteric interpretation of the Hebrew scriptures. A secret doctrine . . ." *American Heritage Dictionary*, 2d college ed., "cabala; cabbala"; "a medieval and modern system of theosophy, mysticism and thaumaturgy (magic)," *Merriam Webster's Collegiate Dictionary* 10th ed., s.v. "cabala."

19. Pike, *Morals and Dogma*, 224.

20. Ibid., 166.

# 11

## Masonry and Religion

*And the children of Israel did evil in the sight of the LORD and served Baalim: and they forsook the LORD God of their fathers . . . and followed other gods, of the people that were round about them, and bowed themselves unto them. . . . And they forsook the LORD and served Baal and Ashtoreth.*

—Judges 2:11-13

### 1. Is Masonry a religion?

Yes, although most Masons will deny this, Masonry is indeed a religion. What else could it be, when:

• they meet in temples (and call the largest ones *cathedrals*);

• they open and close each meeting with prayer;

• they have an altar with a "holy book" opened on it;

• they have deacons;

• they call their leaders such things as "Worshipful Master" and "High Priest";

• they claim to bring the initiate from spiritual darkness to spiritual light;

• they present a plan of salvation and cleansing from sin; and,

• in some degrees, they serve communion and baptize one another?

How, if one examines the evidence at all, could Masonry *not* be a religion?

## 2. How then do Masons deny that Masonry is a religion?

They manage it with typically Masonic double talk. The most common argument is that "We are an order of religious men, but not a religion." (In the same way, they deny being a secret society, saying, "We are a society with secrets, but not a secret society.")

## 3. Do they really believe this?

Yes, they do, at least most of them do. Even though their position holds no water when the evidence is examined, most are sincere when they say that Masonry is not a religion.

## 4. How can they be so wrong and still be sincere?

There are two principal reasons. First, most of them belong to a denomination of some kind, and even though they may seldom or never go to church, to consciously embrace "another religion" would to them seem a betrayal. Second, they believe it because they were told upon entering the Lodge that, whatever their religion, Masonry would not conflict with or contradict it. They believed this because sincere men told them so. Those sincere men who told them so believed it because an earlier generation of sincere men had told them the very same thing. And so, this deception, which originated as a lie in Masonry's dark beginnings, is perpetuated generation after generation.

## 5. What is your basis for saying that Masonry is a religion?

The answer to question 1, above, should suffice, but there is more.

It is common knowledge (at least among those who bother to take notice) that many Masons lose interest in church (if they ever had any such interest) and cease to attend. When asked about it, or urged to attend, they will usually reply, "I don't need to go to church; the Lodge is a good enough religion for me."

This, I believe, is powerful evidence that Masons are taught, one way or another, that Masonry is not only a religion, but the best, and that the Lodge will meet all their spiritual needs, including salvation. If such teachings, explicit and implicit, didn't run through Masonic ritual and instruction, such a widespread belief by sincere men would not be possible. The result, well known within the Lodge and without, is valid and powerful evidence of the process.

But, in addition to this interesting feature of Masonic culture, Masonry's most respected teachers and writers of doctrine themselves identify Masonry as a religion.

> Every Masonic Lodge is a temple of religion; and its teachings are instruction in religion.[1]

> These two essentials, belief in a Supreme being and reverence for his Word, establish beyond question the character of the fraternity as a religious institution.[2]

> A meeting of a Masonic lodge is a religious ceremony.[3]

> The candidate . . . is shown through the Kabalah or Secret Doctrine that, at the heart of every great religion, lie the same eternal truths . . . Masonry is not only a universal science, but a world-wide religion. . . . Masonry is the Universal Religion. . . .[4]

> But the religion of Masonry is not sectarian. It admits men of every creed within its hospitable bosom, rejecting none and approving none for his peculiar faith.[5]

## 6. Does Masonry have any form of a priesthood?

Absolutely; although there is no single priesthood to which some Masons are ordained, there are several forms of priesthood in the order, both functional and symbolic. For example, the title of the leader in the local lodge (Blue Lodge) is "Worshipful Master," and, according to Masonic teachings, "The Master of the Lodge is its priest, and the director of its religious ceremonies."[6]

In addition, the Worshipful Master in the Blue Lodge, when officiating at a Masonic funeral, assumes the role of "High Priest." In the Royal Arch chapter, the presiding officer's (leader's) title is "High Priest." According to the doctrine, he is "the representative of Joshua, the High Priest who, with Zerubbabel, Prince of Judah, and Haggai, the Scribe, laid the foundations of the second temple. . . ."[7] In the Nineteenth Degree (Grand Pontiff) of the Scottish Rite, the candidate is anointed with oil, and it is declared, "Be thou a priest forever, after the order of Melchizedek." In the Thirty-second Degree of Scottish Rite Masonry (Sublime Prince of the Royal Secret), the initiate is again anointed with oil, and it is declared, "Thou art a priest and a prophet."[8]

## 7. Does Masonry present to the initiate a plan of salvation?

Yes, it does over and over. Although there may be no single document entitled "Masonic Plan of Salvation" bearing the imprimatur of a World Headquarters of Freemasonry, there might as well be. Over and over, in Masonic degrees, lessons, ritual, and revered source books, there is clearly expressed a plan of salvation. As is the case with most of Masonry, there are some internal contradictions, but the basic concept is well established, and only the most indifferent or spiritually blinded could miss it.

## 8. If there is a Masonic plan of salvation, what is it?

The Masonic plan of salvation is a three-part plan of self-redemption. The Mason is redeemed (made spiritually perfect and sinless) by (a) being enlightened (having both secret knowledge and the proper understanding of it), (b) faithfulness to his oaths of obligation (death oaths), and (c) his virtuous life (by "being good"). Each man's salvation is his own responsibility; he is his own savior.

Although Masonry promises, from the very first degree, to bring the candidate to "the light," ultimately he must find the light himself. This to me is extremely interesting. In the climactic moment of the Thirty-second Degree, when the candidate has finally reached the top of the Masonic mountain, he is told that the mountain top is covered with mist and clouds, that the light is out there somewhere, and that he must find it for himself. After all that memorizing and stress in the Blue Lodge, after all the time and money spent there and in the Scottish Rite initiations, being promised at every step that he would be brought to the light, he is finally told that he still isn't there and that he will have to find it on his own. This seems like a terrible deception and an outrageous ripoff!

Added to and underlying the basic plan of Masonic salvation, there is reincarnation. Although not prominently displayed, reincarnation is a part of Masonic teaching, appearing especially in the Scottish Rite. By means of this doctrine, the individual goes through an indefinite cycle of lives (incarnations), dying and being reborn for another life, becoming a little more "perfect" in each incarnation (life), or at least having the opportunity to do so, until he finally becomes "perfect."

## 9. What is your basis for saying these things?

On the basis, once again, of the ritual, teachings, and the writings of the most revered Masonic authorities:

> May we be received into Thine everlasting kingdom, to enjoy, in union with the souls of our departed friends, the just reward of a pious and virtuous life. Amen. So mote it be.[9]

> Acacian: a term signifying a mason who by living in strict obedience to obligations and precepts of the fraternity is free from sin.[10]

> Worshipful Master: "In your present, blind condition, what do you most desire?" Initiate to First Degree: "Light."

> Priest (in the Shrine initiation): "Our Oriental will now conduct the Sons of the Desert to our purifying cavern in the South. It is the fountain of Mecca.

Let them there wash their hands in innocency,
cleansing themselves of the snares of sin and vice
that may have surrounded them, and let them be
returned to us free from the stains of iniquity."

Initiation and regeneration are synonymous terms.[11]

I [Masonry] am a way of common men to God.[12]

This principle of Brotherhood and the perfectibility of man's nature through evolution necessitate
Reincarnation . . . all conditions in each life being
determined by previous living.[13]

## 10. Does Masonry view all candidates for initiation as unregenerate sinners when they come to the Lodge?

Yes; all non-Masons are considered "profane" (unclean).
In Albert Mackey's *Manual of the Lodge*, he says:

There he stands without our portals, on the thresh-
old of the new Masonic life, in darkness, helpless-
ness, and ignorance. Having been wandering amid
the errors and covered with the pollutions of the
outer and profane world, he comes inquiringly to
our doors seeking the new birth.[14]

Even professing Christians, ministers, priests, and rabbis are declared unclean and must get on their knees,
confess their lost and polluted condition, and call on the
Worshipful Master and the lodge to bring them out of
deepest spiritual darkness and into the new birth of enlightenment!

## 11. How does Masonry view other religions?

Masonry sees all religions as being only very imperfect
remnants of the ancient pagan mystery religions, distorted
and changed for the worse through the ages, until they
have lost most of their validity and value. It even sees itself
as by far the best of them all and the only hope for

regaining the grandeur and perfection of the "real thing," the ancient mysteries.

> Drop the theological barnacles from the religion of Jesus, as taught by Him, and by the Essenes and Gnostics of the first centuries, and it becomes Masonry. Masonry in its purity, derived as it is from the old Hebrew Kabalah as part of the Great Universal Wisdom-Religion of remotest antiquity.[15]

> Though Masonry is identical with the ancient Mysteries, it is so only in this qualified sense: that it presents but an imperfect image of their brilliancy, the ruins only of their grandeur . . . (its) alterations the fruits of . . . the ambitious imbecility of its improvers.[16]

## 12. Does Masonry have a vision for a world religion?

Yes. If you consider all the Masonic teachings and expressions of doctrine and put them all together, the clear conclusion is that Masonry's goal is to recover the ancient pagan mystery religion, restore it to its original "purity," and unite all mankind around its altar. *The Kentucky Monitor* expresses it thusly: "It [Masonry] makes no profession of Christianity, and wars not against sectarian creeds or doctrines, but looks forward to the time when . . . there shall be but one altar, one worship, one common altar of Masonry. . . ."[17]

Of course, there is a problem here, a very great problem. That problem is that only "good" men can be admitted to this ultimate, perfect religion once it is rediscovered, leaving no hope of redemption for women, children, and "bad" men. But, perhaps reincarnation can take care of this, with the "bad" men eventually becoming "good," and the women and children eventually becoming men.

---

## Endnotes

1. Albert Pike, *Morals and Dogma,* rev. ed. (Washington, DC: House of the Temple, 1950), 113.

2. Joseph Fort Newton, "The Great Light of Masonry," *Masonic Bible* (A. J. Holmes Co., 1968), unnumbered page.

3. "Chaplain," *Webb's Freemason's Monitor* (LaGrange, KY: Rob Morris Publishers, 1862), 231.

4. J.D. Buck, *Mystic Masonry,* 3rd ed. (Chicago: Chas T. Powner Publishing Co., 1925), 46, 47.

5. Albert Mackey, *Encyclopedia of Freemasonry*, rev. ed. s.v. "religion" (Chicago, New York, London: Masonic History Co., 1927), 619.

6. Webb, *Freemason's Monitor,* 280.

7. Albert Mackey, *Lexicon of Freemasonry*, 2nd Ed., s.v. "high priest" (Charleston, SC: Walker and James, 1852), 195.

8. J. Blanchard, *Scottish Rite Masonry, Illustrated*, vol II (Chicago: Chas T. Powner Publishing Co., 1972), 26.

9. M. Taylor, "Masonic Burial Service,"*Texas Monitor* (Houston, TX: Grand Lodge of Texas, 1883), 147.

10. Albert Mackey, *Lexicon of Freemasonry,* 2nd ed., s.v. "acacian."

11. Buck, *Mystic Masonry,* 44.

12. Carl Claudy, "Spirit of Masonry" *The Kentucky Monitor* (Louisville, KY: Standard Printing Co., 1921), xx, xxi.

13. Buck, *Mystic Masonry,* 63.

14. Albert Mackey, *Manual of the Lodge* (New York: MaCoy Publishing Co., 1903), 22-23.

15. Buck, *Mystic Masonry,* 66-67.

16. Pike, *Morals and Dogma,* 23.

17. Henry Pirtle,*The Kentucky Monitor* (Louisville, KY: Standard Printing Co., 1921), 95.

# 12

## Masonry's Exclusiveness and Elitism

*And the Spirit and the bride say come. . . . And let him that is athirst come. And whosoever will, let him take the water of life freely.*

—Revelation 22:17

*And ye masters [remember] that your Master also is in Heaven; neither is there any respect of persons with Him.*

—Ephesians 6:9

### 1. Is Masonry open to anyone who wants to join?

Absolutely not! Exclusiveness has been a hallmark of Freemasonry since its earliest beginnings. Socially, it was founded by English aristocrats and was open to the socially elite; the first Grand Master (1717) is identified in the records as "Anthony Sayer, Gentleman," not "Anthony Sayer, Bricklayer."

Spiritually, the mystery religions, the roots of Masonry, have always been for only an elite, favored few. These elite insiders were the only ones with the knowledge of the secrets, the secrets were the keys to power, and they only admitted those to their elite group who had been chosen and initiated.

The social snobbery may be offensive, but it is harmless. The spiritual snobbery is a much more serious matter.

## 2. Then, does a man have to be an aristocrat in order to join the Masonic Lodge today?

No, definitely not, or their numbers would be very much smaller than they are; but, the principle of elitism and exclusiveness prevails throughout the system.

In England, the high offices are still occupied by the aristocracy, and the office of Grand Master is often occupied by a member of the royal family. The current Grand Master is His Royal Highness, the Duke of Kent. Yet, even in England, men of ordinary means and humble birth may today be admitted to the Lodge (although they will seldom, if ever, achieve high office).

In the United States, men of very humble birth and little education are readily taken into the Lodge, but the same "snob factor" prevails throughout the system. Those of wealth and prominence definitely have the edge, and an honest Mason will tell you this. There are some offices, and even some organizations, in American Masonry which the "ordinary" Masons will never achieve. As George Orwell wrote in *Animal Farm*, "All animals are equal; but some are more equal than others."

This is especially true of the Shrine, which accepts only Masons of the Thirty-second Degree in the Scottish Rite or Knight Templar degree in the York Rite. In the Shrine, even the local leader (Illustrious Potentate) is expected to have the wealth and position to be socially active and sufficiently impressive to visiting dignitaries. No matter how hard a man may work, no matter how totally committed he may be, if he doesn't have money, a nice home, social position, etc., he will probably never occupy high office in the Shrine.

In fact, there are even some Masonic organizations with such a high "snob factor" that he will not be allowed to join; some of the most prestigious auxiliary groups in the Shrine are "by invitation only." It seems unbelievable, but a Shriner may have to spend more than one hundred thousand dollars to be elected to the national leadership's

"Imperial Divan." (See chapter 5.) This excludes thousands of Masons from even hoping to rise to leadership.

## 3. Who then may join the Lodge?

To summarize, Freemasonry is open only to men (no women may be initiated) who are "good" ("of good report"), who are "freeborn" (neither born in slavery or bondservice, nor the son of such a person not born free), white, without physical disability, without mental impairment or emotional sickness, who have the money required, who are "of full age" (twenty-one or older) but not "old," and not an atheist.[1]

## 4. Are these restrictions on membership literally true?

Yes. One of the things a Master Mason swears to, on penalty of mutilation and death, is that he will not take part in the initiation of a "clandestine" Mason (a black or a woman), "a young man in his nonage" (underage), or "an old man in his dotage" (feeble, senile, or simply old), or one emotionally disturbed or mentally ill ("a madman or a fool").[2]

When the candidate for the first degree is presented for initiation, the Junior Deacon is asked of the candidate's qualifications "to gain admission" to the Lodge. He answers, "By being a man, freeborn, white and of full age."[3]

## 5. How do Masons justify this exclusiveness?

They can't, and they don't like being asked about it. When they are asked about their exclusion of certain types of people, they will usually react as they do to other negative aspects of Masonry: they will either deny it or say that they are not allowed to discuss it. It's either, "It isn't so," or "I can't talk about that."

## 6. Why does Masonry exclude these kinds of people?

In terms of their basic policy of exclusiveness ("We make good men better"), it seems to be traceable to

Masonry's beginnings as an order for just the well born, well educated, and reputable. This, I believe, is the origin of their exclusiveness in social terms. But, in a way much more sinister, their exclusiveness is readily traceable to the pagan mystery religions with secret initiations and elite priesthoods, the spiritual and ceremonial roots of Masonry.

## 7. Is there any practical reason for their excluding these people?

Yes and no. They exclude women and blacks simply because they consider them unsuitable or undesirable. They exclude the deaf because they can't hear the passwords, recognition, and distress signs. They exclude the physically disabled—amputees, paralytics—because they can't assume the proper body positions for dueguards, penalty signs, etc. They exclude the blind because they can't see the dueguards, penalty signs, etc. They exclude the poor because they can't pay or occupy too low a level in society. They exclude the emotionally troubled because they can't be trusted with their secrets. And, they exclude (at least theoretically) the sinner because their system is only for "good" men who want to be made better.

## 8. What is so wrong about this?

Early in my study of Masonry, it occurred to me that these groups which Masonry automatically rejects are the groups that Jesus went after. He sought out sinners in general, and his time and energy were primarily expended on the unwanted, the blind, the deaf, the crippled, the poor, and the emotionally disturbed. These people, who need not even apply to the Masonic Lodge, were the ones in which Jesus specialized, those to whom He most readily opened His arms and said, "Come unto me."

I find this contrast extremely interesting and enormously significant.

## 9. But, still, if some men want to have an organization for social reasons and limit its membership only to certain people or types of people, isn't that their right?

Absolutely. I believe strongly in the right of association (or nonassociation). I believe that if it is merely a social organization or club and its policy is to accept into their membership only left-handed white men with red hair and blue eyes who are graduates of MIT in odd-numbered years (make up any set of restrictions you like here, the principle is the same), the organization should have every right to do so. Even if they want to consider themselves superior to the rest of us, that's perfectly alright with me. I couldn't care less.

Not only is the right to free association a hallmark of free societies, it is also a scriptural principle that two cannot "walk together except they be agreed" (Amos 3:3).

## 10. Then, what's so wrong with Masonry for accepting only certain types of people?

What makes this question different with Masonry is that it presents itself as a means of spiritual redemption. Philosophically and logically, it is indefensible to declare on the one hand, "We are the only ones with the true spiritual light, the only ones with the truth," and then to say on the other hand, "What we have is not for everyone." It is like saying, "I am the man on the ship with the life preservers; but when the ship sinks, I'm only going to give them to a few of my friends."

## 11. Why does Masonry reject blacks?

This exclusion undoubtedly has its beginnings in the prevailing social and political attitudes and customs at the time of Masonry's origin in eighteenth century England, continuing into its spread into the American colonies. Blacks were looked upon as being inferior and socially unacceptable.

## 12. But, how do Masons justify this form of racial discrimination today?

They usually don't try to. When confronted with Masonry's historic rejection of blacks, most Masons will deny it and say that there are blacks in Masonry. But, what they are referring to (although they won't want to tell you) is the entirely separate black Masonic system called "Prince Hall" Masonry.

## 13. What is Prince Hall Masonry?

Prince Hall Masonry is the Masonic system for blacks. It is exactly like "white" Masonry, with the same rituals, same "secrets," all the same systems for higher degrees; it has its own Shrine and the same "adoptive" orders (e.g., Eastern Star, Rainbow Girls, etc.). It also has its own problems, including the same pagan roots.

## 14. Doesn't this mean that Masonry is open to blacks?

Definitely not; Freemasonry (the "legitimate" system) looks upon Prince Hall Masonry as counterfeit, an illegitimate imitation of the real thing. Prince Hall Masonry is classified as "clandestine" Masonry, one of the things in which a Master Mason swears to take no part, under penalty of death.

## 15. How did Prince Hall Masonry come to exist?

It all seems to have begun with a black named Prince Hall. The exact history is hazy, but it is probably true that the British army, for reasons of its own, authorized Prince Hall and thirteen other black men to organize a lodge called "African Lodge," in Boston. This lodge, not recognized by the Grand Lodge of Massachusetts, refused to acknowledge any allegiance to that Grand Lodge and continued to operate in some form until the death of Prince Hall and his colleagues. In 1827, the system was revived. Receiving no recognition from the Grand Lodge of England, the men decided to acknowledge no Masonic authority but their own. They decided that "with what knowledge they possessed of Masonry, and as people of color by themselves, they were, and ought by rights to be, free and independent of other Lodges." From this beginning, a complete Masonic system developed and spread to Canada, Liberia, and other foreign countries.

This elaborate Masonic system, a perfect parallel with white, "legitimate" Masonry, is still classified as illegitimate, clandestine, and off-limits to all white Masons. Albert Mackey, one of the most important Masonic writers of doctrine, summed it up thusly:

> It cannot be denied that the unrecognized self-revival of 1827, and the subsequent assumption of Grand Lodge powers, were illegal and rendered both the Prince Hall Grand Lodge and all the Lodges which emanated from it clandestine. And this has been the unanimous opinion of all Masonic Jurists in America.[4]

It is interesting, but not surprising, that the same attitude of superiority and spirit of snobbery exist among Prince Hall Masons toward those blacks outside the Lodge system which has prevailed among white Masons towards blacks and others outside its confines. People are, after all, people.

## 16. Are there ever exceptions in local lodges to these rules of exclusion in membership?

Yes, there are, but they are definitely exceptions and not the rule. I was told by one Mason in New York that his lodge had taken in a black man, and I'm sure that it has happened elsewhere. Because of changes in social mores and political pressures, change seems inevitable, and the resulting social adjustments will be increasingly painful, emotional, and divisive. Looming before Masonry, as a whole, is a growing problem of enormous proportions.

For example, the Grand Lodge of West Virginia recently issued an edict "forbidding members of the Most

Worshipful Grand Lodge of West Virginia, Ancient Free
and Accepted Masons to visit lodges under the Grand
Lodges" of seven northern and western states because of
their openness to recognizing Prince Hall Masonry as
legitimate.[5]

## 17. Are there ever exceptions to the other exclusions for membership in the local lodge?

Yes, or at least so I am told, and I am inclined to
believe it. A man called me on one talk show and told me
that he was a Mason, although he was blind, and had been
blind when taken into the lodge. Another man called on
another such broadcast and told me that his lodge had
taken in a man in a wheelchair. But, I emphasize, these are
exceptions and not the rule. Once a local lodge has taken
in such a man, initiated him, and given him the "secrets"
of a Master Mason, the Grand Lodge is presented with a
*fait accompli* and has no choice but to allow him to stay.

Concerning the poor, there are definitely cases in
which a man who cannot afford the initiation fees will
have them paid for him by a member of the lodge, in
order to be able to take him in. But, such a man will be
expected to stand on his own financial feet from that time
on. Again, such cases are the exception and not the rule.
There is a cost to entering and remaining in the Lodge.

## 18. Do you know of any men who have been denied membership because of disability?

Yes, several. One man I remember was blinded as a
marine in the battle for Iwo Jima in World War II. When
he returned to civilian life, he applied for membership in
his local lodge. He was rejected because of his blindness.

The most poignant and powerful example of this that
I know is that of a man in Tampa, Florida. He had grown
up in a Masonic family, had been an ardent member of
the Order of DeMolay, had gone through the chairs and
held all its offices, and loved it. He was living for the day
when he would reach his twenty-first birthday so he could

enter the Lodge. When he was nineteen, he was drafted into the army and sent to Korea, where he was terribly wounded, bayoneted, and left by the enemy for dead. He survived but was blinded, lost one leg, and one arm was paralyzed. By the time he recovered from his wounds and returned home, he was twenty-one. He immediately petitioned his local lodge for membership, the fulfillment of his lifelong dream, and was summarily rejected because of his disabilities. He told me that, at the time, this rejection by the Masonic system he so loved hurt him more than all his physical wounds. Now, he is a Christian and says that their rejection of him was his gain and their loss.

## 19. But, what about women; are they ever taken into the Lodge?

Never. To my knowledge, this is the exception never made, which is interesting. With the exception of Mrs. Aldworth (Elizabeth St. Leger) and a few other bizarre and questionable cases, including Annie Besant, famed English mystic, occultist, and socialist, Masonic history is consistent and emphatic: women have never been admitted to Freemasonry. (See Appendix A, "Female 'Brothers' in the Lodge.") "Androgynous" Masonry, including both women and men, has been largely a French idea, as has been the case of purely female Masonry; neither has ever found acceptance by Freemasonry in general.

English Freemasonry (along with its American, European, and Asian offsprings) has from its earliest beginnings excluded women.[6] This "ancient landmark" has never been shaken. Most Masons won't know why this has always been done, and those who are familiar with the argument will tell you that it is because the work of operative stonemasons (the real ones, from which they draw much of their symbolism) required the physical strength of men, and speculative Masons (the guys in the Lodge) have carried on their ancient tradition of excluding women. The truth may be much darker, as explained in Appendix A.

## 20. What is meant by the Masonic expression "profane world"?

This is an extremely important question; one that goes to the heart of Masonic exclusiveness and elitism. The word *profane* derives from the Latin word *profanus* meaning "outside, or excluded from, the Temple." The expanded meaning refers to one who is unclean, polluted, unholy, and entirely unacceptable. In Masonic teachings, anyone not an initiated Mason is *profane*, and there is frequent reference in their ritual and conversations to "the profane" (people) or "the profane world," meaning all the non-Masonic world around them.

Here is still another thing most Masons seem never to think of, but this doctrine of basic snobbery means that their wives, mothers, daughters, and grandmothers are all "unclean and unfit for fellowship." So also are their sons, fathers, brothers, and grandfathers if not Masons. This is worth pondering.

---

## Endnotes

1. Albert Mackey, *Jurisprudence of Freemasonry*, rev. and enlarged ed. Book II (Chicago: Chas T. Powner Co., 1975), 14; Henry W. Coil, *Masonic Encyclopedia* (New York: MaCoy Publishing Co., 1961), 494-496.

2. Malcolm C. Duncan, *Ducan's Masonic Ritual and Monitor*, 3rd ed. (New York: David McKay Co., undated), 94-96.

3. Ibid., 28-29; this response is modified today in some parts of the country to "By being a man, freeborn, of a full age and of a good reputation." In the South, the original wording is still common.

4. Albert Mackey, *Encyclopedia of Freemasonry*, rev. ed. s.v. (Chicago, New York, London: Masonic History Co., 1927), 508, 509.

5. Connecticut, Wisconsin, Nebraska, Washington, Colorado, Minnesota, and North Dakota.

6. The charges compiled by Anderson and Desaguliers (founders of speculative Masonry) were explicit in this regard: "the persons admitted members of a Lodge must be good and true men." Mackey, *Encyclopedia of Freemasonry*, s.v. "woman," 855.

# 13

# Masonry and Jesus Christ

*Whosoever denieth the Son, the same hath not the Father.*
—1 John 3:23

## 1. Does Masonry acknowledge Jesus as Lord and Savior?

The answer to this question is what propelled me into the study of Freemasonry twenty years ago. As I reluctantly began to read the introduction to *The Kentucky Monitor*, a "secret" Masonic book, in order to please a friend, it immediately got my attention, aroused my interest, then nearly knocked me off my chair!

My first "Masonic shock" was learning that Masonry is not just a fraternal order given to good works but is, in fact, a revival of the pagan mystery religions of Egypt and the East.[1]

My second "Masonic shock" was learning that Masonry denies the divinity and uniqueness of Jesus, equating Him to "other saviors" of history.[2]

My third and greatest "Masonic shock" was learning that Masonry has its own messiah, someone called "Hiram."[3]

## 2. Then, where does Jesus fit into the Masonic system and doctrine?

He is presented as just one of what they call the "exemplars," the great men of the past, on the same level with

Buddha, Confucious, Mohammed, and Aristotle. Listen to the words of Albert Pike:

> It (Masonry) reverences all the great reformers. It sees Moses, the lawgiver to the Jews, in Confucious and Zoroaster, in Jesus of Nazareth, and in the Arabian Iconoclast (Mohammed), great teachers of morality, and eminent reformers, if no more.[4]

As a matter of fact, when we consider the Shrine, Masonry views Jesus to be even lower than the other "exemplars" because, in Islam, Jesus is recognized as only a minor prophet, decidedly inferior to Mohammed.

## 3. Is this true, even in Lodges where all or most of the members are Christian?

Definitely; of course, many who would classify themselves as Christians may not be truly born-again into the family of God. (I was such a nominal Christian for most of my life.) But, even if every member of a local Lodge were born-again Christians, it wouldn't change in any way the status of Jesus in their Lodge. He could not be honored as the unique Savior of lost mankind, nor could prayers be offered in His name. Masonic doctrine is Masonic doctrine, regardless of the religious persuasion of a Lodge's membership.

## 4. Do you mean that Masons are not allowed to honor Jesus as Lord in the Lodge?

Not out loud, some of them may truly honor Him in their hearts, but they are not allowed in any way to acknowledge Him outwardly as Lord in the Lodge.

## 5. Why is this so?

Because, very simply, Freemasonry is not Christian. In addition, as the usual justification goes, it would be offensive to the non-Christians in the Lodge. Some Lodges have a mix of Christians, Deists, Mormons, Muslims, etc., and the principle is that they must not be offended by having Jesus honored as Lord.

In a classic example of this Masonic syncretism, my friend Mick Oxley, while an officer in the Royal Air Force, belonged to a lodge in Singapore under the English Constitutions (chartered by the United Grand Lodge of England) in which the Worshipful Master was a Muslim, the Senior Warden was a Muslim, the Junior Warden was a Hindu, the Senior Deacon was a Hindu, the Junior Deacon was a Taoist, and the Tiler was a Sikh.

## 6. But, doesn't this make sense? Shouldn't the Christian Masons be tolerant of their non-Christian brothers?

In human terms, this seems reasonable and right; but, from a scriptural point of view, it is very wrong. To fail to acknowledge and confess Jesus is to deny Him, and to deny Him is a spiritually fatal error.

As a matter of fact, Christians shouldn't even have "non-Christian brothers" because of the scriptural admonition not to be unequally yoked with unbelievers; nor are we to have fellowship with the unfruitful works of darkness.[5] And, in the Lodge, Christians are not just associating with unbelievers in social functions and community service, they are literally bound together with them by "unbreakable" death oaths, sworn to give them unfair preference in all dealings and to conceal their crimes. (See chapter 17, "Death Oaths and Masonic Execution.")

For those who would seek refuge behind the defense that they only belong to a local lodge whose members are all Christians, I point out that every Mason who has ever taken even the first obligation is bound in brotherhood to every Mason who ever lived.[6]

## 7. Is it true that prayers in the Masonic Lodge are not offered in Jesus' name?

This is definitely true. The prayers of Masonry must be kept "universal" so as not to offend any of the non-Christians in the system. This happens even in the so-called "Christian" degrees of the York Rite. The Reverend

Harmon Taylor is past Grand Chaplain of the Grand Lodge of New York; as such, he was given only one instruction and was given that one many times. This oft-repeated direction was that he was never, under any circumstance, to offer prayers in Masonic gatherings in Jesus' name.[7]

This prohibition also prevails in the Eastern Star, which most of its members believe to be Christian. Even in the Rainbow Girls, the prayers are "universal" and Christless. Their burial service (yes, those little girls really do have one) makes reference to "the master teacher," who could be Aristotle, Zoroaster, or the teacher of the year in Possum Trot, Kentucky—and this is as close as they get to honoring Jesus.

## 8. Are prayers ever offered in Jesus' name in a Masonic Lodge?

Yes. There are sometimes exceptions to this rule, but they are definitely exceptions and not the rule. Let me explain. There are some small town lodges, especially in the South, where this rule is sometimes broken. In such a small town, where all the churches are at least nominally Christian and there is no one offended by such prayer, the chaplain may, in some cases, offer prayer in Jesus' name. However, if a visitor reports it, or in any other way word of this reaches the Grand Lodge headquarters in that state, the local lodge will be forced to stop praying in Jesus' name or have its charter revoked.

## 9. Do you mean that a Masonic Lodge could actually have its charter revoked if its leaders insisted on honoring Jesus in the Lodge or offering prayers in His name?

Yes. This, I think, is an eloquent expression of Masonry's position on Jesus. Masonry is not only non-Christian, but, because it denies His rightful place in the universe, Masonry is actually anti-Christian. Jesus Himself said that those who are not for Him are against Him.

## 10. Do Masons have their own system for reckoning time?

Yes, and it is yet another way in which Jesus is denied in the Lodge. Virtually all the rest of the civilized world counts years from the birth of Jesus, before and since. "B.C." is an abbreviation of the words "before Christ." "A.D." is an abbreviation of the words "Anno Domini," Latin for "in the year of our Lord." Julius Caesar was born 100 B.C.; Jerusalem fell to the Roman General Titus in A.D. 70, and Abraham Lincoln was murdered in A.D. 1865. That's the way most of us reckon time, and I love it because, in so doing, the entire civilized world acknowledges and honors Jesus, even calling Him "our Lord."

But, Freemasonry does not do this—not even in the "Christian" degrees of the York Rite. Masons use a different system, and their system leaves Jesus completely out. In Masonry, current time is reckoned, not from the birth of Jesus, but from the supposed time of creation, 4,000 years B.C. So, Masonic time is reckoned by adding four thousand to the current year and calling it "Anno Lucis" (in the year of light), abbreviated "A.L." By their system, A.D. 1993 becomes A.L. 5993. You may confirm this by looking at the engraved date on any cornerstone laid by Masons.[8]

## 11. Does Masonry teach the need for any personal savior?

No. Concisely and simply stated, Masonry teaches that we must save ourselves by initiation into Freemasonry, by growing in knowledge ("light") through its degrees, by obedience to the oaths of obligation, and by leading a virtuous life ("being good"). To help with all this, there is the doctrine of reincarnation.

Faith is not only not required, but the concept of salvation by faith is considered to be an "ignorant perversion" of the truth, and the Apostles who first taught it "dunces." Nowhere in all Masonic teachings is there declared (or even inferred) a need for basically sinful man to have a personal savior, and if there is even an oblique reference to a personal savior, it is Hiram Abiff not Jesus.[9] And, if one is "redeemed" by Hiram, it is not by faith in him, but by gaining knowledge of him, a very different matter indeed.

## 12. Can you document that amazing statement?

I realize that all this sounds bizarre, especially to the Christian, but let's allow the Masonic philosophers to speak for themselves. Once again, I could fill this book with documentation to this effect, but that obviously would not be workable; a few examples must suffice:

> By the Lambskin [apron] the Mason is reminded of that purity of life and rectitude of conduct which are so essentially necessary to his gaining admission into the Celestial Lodge above ["heaven"], where the Supreme Architect of the Universe presides.[10]

> And in Thy favor may we be received into Thine everlasting kingdom to enjoy, in union with the souls of our departed friends, the just reward of a pious and virtuous life. Amen. So mote it be.[11]

> Acacian: a term signifying a Mason who, by living in strict obedience to the obligations [oaths] and precepts [teachings] of the fraternity, is free from sin.[12]

> The rite of induction signifies the end of a profane and vicious life, the palingenisis [new birth] of corrupt human nature, the death of vice and all bad passions, and the introduction to the new life of purity and virtue.[13]

> These three degrees [first, second, and third] thus form a perfect and harmonious whole, nor can it be conceived that anything can be suggested more, which the soul of man requires.[14]

> Step by step men must advance towards Perfection:

and each Masonic Degree is meant to be one of those steps.[15]

Salvation by faith and the vicarious atonement were not taught as now interpreted by Jesus, nor are these doctrines taught in the esoteric [hidden] scriptures. They are later and ignorant perversions of the original doctrines.[16]

The dunces who led primitive Christianity astray, by substituting faith for science, reverie for experience, the fantastic for the reality; and the inquisitors who for so many ages waged against Magism [magic, sorcery] a war of extermination, have succeeded in shrouding in darkness the ancient discoveries of the human mind.[17]

All antiquity believed . . . in a Mediator or Redeemer, by means of whom the Evil Principle was to be overcome and the Supreme Deity reconciled to His creatures. The belief was general that he was to be born of a virgin and suffer a painful death. The Hindus called him Krishna; the Chinese, Kiountse; the Persians, Sosiosch; the Scandinavians, Balder; the Christians, Jesus; the Masons, Hiram.[18]

It is Christos or Hiram, the Mediator between the soul, or physical man, and the Great Spirit—the Father in Heaven.[19]

It is far more important that men should strive to become Christs than that they should believe that Jesus was Christ.[20]

Theologians . . . tore the Christos from the hearts of all humanity in order to deify Jesus, that they might have a God-man peculiarly their own![21]

In the early church, as in the secret doctrine, there was not a personal Christ for the whole world but a potential Christ in every living being. Hence Masons believe in the Architect of the Universe, but positively not in Jesus the man as the only Son of God.[22]

This principle of Brotherhood and the perfectibility of man's nature through evolution necessitate Reincarnation. . . . Hence the doctrine of pre-existence taught in all the Mysteries applies to "every child of woman born;" all conditions in each life being determined by previous living.[23]

To achieve it [Heaven], the Mason must first attain a solid conviction, founded on reason, that he hath within him a spiritual nature, a soul that is not to die when the body is dissolved, but is to continue to exist and to advance toward perfection through all the ages of eternity. . . . This [Reincarnation] the Philosophy of the Ancient and Accepted Rite teaches him.[24]

In deifying Jesus the whole of humanity is bereft of Christos as an eternal potency within every human soul, a latent Christ in every man. In thus deifying one man, they [the Christians] have orphaned the whole of humanity! On the other hand Masonry, in making every man personify Hiram, has preserved the original teaching. . . . Few candidates may be aware that Hiram whom they have represented and personified, is ideally and precisely the same as Christ. Yet such is undoubtedly the case.[25]

## 13. Does Masonry really teach that Jesus is not unique, but is just one of many "redeemers"?

Absolutely. For openers, see question 12, cite eighteen, above; there, in the introduction to *The Kentucky Monitor*, it is plainly (if a bit obliquely) said that there is really nothing special about Jesus, that all civilizations have had a myth of such a messiah, born of a virgin, suffered, and died, and so on. For more, let's again allow the leading Masonic writers to speak for themselves:

Krishna, the Hindoo Redeemer, was cradled and educated among shepherds. A tyrant, at the time of his birth, ordered all the male children to be slain. He performed miracles, say his legends, even raising the dead. He washed the feet of the Brahmins. It was on a cruciform tree [a cross] that Krishna was said to have expired, pierced with arrows. He descended into Hell, rose again, ascended to Heaven, charged his disciples to teach his doctrines, and gave them the gift of miracles.[26] [Does this sound familiar to you Christians? It should.]

Every act in the drama of the life of Jesus, and every quality assigned to Christ, is to be found in the life of Krishna and in the legend of all the Sun-Gods from the remotest antiquity.[27]

The true Mason is not creed-bound. He realizes with the divine illumination [light] of his lodge that as a Mason his religion must be universal; Christ, Buddha or Mohammed, the name means little, for he recognizes only the light and not the bearer. He worships at every shrine, bows before every altar, whether in temple, mosque or cathedral. . . .[28]

In his private devotions, a man may petition God or Jehovah, Allah, or Buddha, Mohammed or Jesus; he may call upon the God of Israel or the First Great Cause. . . . A hundred paths may wind upward around a mountain; at the top they meet.[29]

Is Jesus any the less Christos because Christna was called "The Good Shepherd?" or because the Mexican Christ was crucified between two thieves? or because Hiram was three days in a grave before he was resurrected?[30]

## 14. Who is this Hiram who seems to be so important in Masonry?

Hiram Abiff is the central character in the legend of the third degree of the Blue Lodge; as such, he is the most important person in Blue Lodge Masonry. According to Masonic tradition, Hiram was the chief architect in the building of the temple in Jerusalem by King Solomon. He is called "Hiram, the Widow's son" and is a mythological character consisting of a mixture of fact and fiction.

There are two Hirams in the scriptural account of the building of Solomon's Temple: Hiram, King of Tyre, friend of King David and of his son, King Solomon, who provided much of the material for the temple's construction; and Hiram, a widow's son, of the tribe of Naphtali, a worker in metals, who was brought to the construction project by King Hiram to make the vessels of brass. This real Hiram, a remarkable craftsman and artist, made all the wonderful brass objects and implements for the temple, "made an end of all his work" for the temple, and apparently went back home and lived happily ever after.[31]

The Hiram of Masonic legend is supposed to have been the chief architect of the temple project. He was also, in some way, a master mason, and the "grand master" of all the stonemasons working on the temple. The story is (typically) confused because Hiram is called "our first Grand Master," yet both King Solomon and King Hiram are also referred to as grand masters. Nevertheless, as the story goes, Hiram knew the "Master's Word," a secret the working masons wouldn't be qualified to receive until the temple was finished. Several of the masons ("ruffians") decided that they wanted to know the word before they finished, and trying to scare or beat the secret out of Hiram, they ultimately killed him. After three days the truth was revealed, the "ruffians" were caught, and the grave was opened. King Solomon, with Masonic technique, raises Hiram from the dead. This, in greatly abbreviated form, is the legend of Hiram Abiff.

## 15. But, what does this have to do with Jesus?

Everything—or nothing at all—depending on how one views it. In the climactic part of the third degree initiation, the legend of Hiram is enacted as a play in the lodge hall, with the bewildered, hoodwinked candidate playing the role of Hiram. As is the case with all the rest of his initiations, the candidate knows nothing of this in advance. (In fact, he has already been led to believe that his initiation is finished, then he must again take off his clothes and be rehoodwinked.) He is led through the bewildering skit, about which he knows nothing, being jerked around by three consecutive "ruffians" (who really do get rough), is "buried" under "rubble of the Temple," and then resurrected by the Worshipful Master, playing the role of Solomon.

Almost none of this is scriptural, almost none of it is true, and some of it is downright blasphemous. God Himself was the architect of the temple, laying down plans and specifications to the last minute detail. And, there was no "rubble" in the building of the temple; every stone was cut to fit at a distant site and merely put in place in the temple. And, what is even more outrageous, in the legend, Hiram takes his lunch break in the Holy of Holies! All serious Masonic historians acknowledge that it is pure myth and legend; yet, most Masons believe that it is all true. The shock effect, confusion, and fear leave the hoodwinked candidate vulnerable to deep spiritual bondage.

Here is how it relates to Jesus. Hiram Abiff actually represents Osiris, the Egyptian sun and sex god. In order to receive the Masonic "new birth" and ascend from spiritual darkness to light, the candidate must enter into the death, burial, and resurrection of Hiram Abiff (Osiris), Masonry's bogus redeemer. To quote just one of the Masonic philosophers, "In the third degree the candidate impersonates Hiram, who has been shown to be identical with Christos of the Greeks, and with the Sun-Gods of all other nations."[32]

This is a blasphemous parody of genuine redemption by faith in Christ Jesus.

(If you would like to know more about the legend of Hiram Abiff, how it relates to Isis and Osiris, its real spiritual implications, and what Masonic scholars say about it, see the Huntington House book, *Deadly Deception*, Appendix D, by the author and Jim Shaw.)

## Endnotes

1. Henry Pirtle, "The Spirit of Masonry," *The Kentucky Monitor* (Louisville, KY: Standard Printing Co., 1921), xi, xii.

2. Ibid., xiv, xv.

3. Ibid., xv.

4. Albert Pike, *Morals and Dogma,* rev. ed. (Washington, DC: House of the Temple, 1950), 525.

5. 2 Corinthians 6:14-18; Ephesians 5:6-11.

6. Albert Pike, *Morals and Dogma,* 726.

7. Harmon R. Taylor, *Oil and Water* (Newtonville, NY: HRT Ministries, undated pamphlet; Personal Interview, Knoxville, TN: 5 June 1993).

8. Here again there is contradiction and confusion in Masonry. Blue Lodge Masonry uses this basic system (Anno Lucis); the York Rite uses another (Anno Ordinis, "the Year of the Order," dating from the year 1118, which is subtracted from the A.D. year); the Scottish Rite uses still another (Anno Mundi, "the Year of the World," adding 3,760 to the A.D. year, approximately the same as the Jewish system); and there are even more!

9. Pirtle, *The Kentucky Monitor,* xv; J.D. Buck, *Mystic Masonry,* 3rd ed. (Chicago: Chas T. Powner Co., 1925), 133.

10. Albert Mackey, *Encyclopedia of Freemasonry,* rev ed. s.v. "apron," (Chicago, New York, London: Masonic History Co., 1927), 72-74.

11. M. Taylor, "Masonic Burial Service," *Texas Monitor* (Houston, TX: Grand Lodge of Texas, 1883), 147.

12. Albert Mackey, *Lexicon of Freemasonry,* 2nd ed., s.v. "Acacian," 6.

13. Daniel Sickles, *Ahiman Rhezon and Freemason's Guide* (New York: MaCoy Publishing Co., 1911), 54.

14. Ibid., 196.

15. Pike, *Morals and Dogma,* 136.

16. Buck, *Mystic,* 57.

17. Pike, *Morals and Dogma*, 732.

18. Pirtle, *Kentucky Monitor*, 14, 15.

19. Buck, *Mystic*, 45.

20. Ibid., p 62.

21. Ibid., p 57.

22. Ibid.

23. Ibid., 63; S.R. Parchment, *Ancient Operative Masonry* (San Francisco: San Francisco Center-Rosicrucian Fellowship, 1930), 35.

24. Pike, *Morals and Dogma*, 855.

25. Buck, *Mystic*, 63.

26. Pirtle, *Kentucky Monitor*, xv.

27. Buck, *Mystic*, 63.

28. Manley P. Hall, *The Lost Keys of Freemasonry* (Richmond, VA: MaCoy Publishing Co., 1976), 65.

29. Carl H. Claudy, *Introduction to Freemasonry* (Washington, DC: Temple Publishers, 1939), 38.

30. Buck, *Mystic*, 47.

31. 1 Kings 7:13-40.

32. Buck, *Mystic*, 133.

This Methodist church in Dundee, Kentucky, was converted into a Masonic lodge hall and meeting place for the Order of the Eastern Star. Notice the goat on the steeple in place of a cross.

# 14

# Masonry and Secrecy

*I [Jesus] spake openly to the world; I ever taught in the synagogue and in the temple . . . and in secret have I said nothing.*

—John 18:20

## 1. Why do Masons seem so mysterious and secretive about what they do?

They are so mysterious and secretive because secrecy has been a basic characteristic of Freemasonry since its founding. As a matter of fact, this is part of its foundational law, one of its "landmarks." (See question 7, below.) This is the feature that makes Masonry appealing to many Masons; they enjoy being part of an exclusive group with secrets that others "aren't in on."

## 2. Why has Masonry been secretive since its beginnings?

The secrecy has remained entrenched for two reasons. First, the medieval stonemasons' guilds, from which Masonry takes so much of its symbolism, met in secret in order to protect their trade secrets.

Second, and more important, Masonry is based on and is a revival of the ancient pagan mystery religions of the East, especially those of Egypt. The ancient mysteries were for only an elite few; secrecy and exclusiveness were characteristic. According to the *Encyclopedia of Freemasonry* (s.v., "ancient mysteries"), they were:

> the secret worship rites of the Pagan gods. Each of the Pagan gods had, besides the public and open, a secret worship paid to him, to which none were admitted but those who had been selected by preparatory ceremonies called Initiation.

Concerning those mystery religions, the *Encyclopedia* goes on to say,

> Secret ceremonies were practised in honor of certain gods, and whose secret was known to the initiates alone, who were admitted only after long and painful trials, which it was more than their life was worth to reveal. . . . The most important of these mysteries were the Osiric [those of Osiris and Isis] in Egypt.[1]

## 3. Is Masonry a secret society?

Absolutely; according to the *Encyclopaedia Britannica*, Freemasonry is not only a secret society but the world's largest.[2]

## 4. Do Masons ever deny that theirs is a secret society?

Yes, they will almost always deny being a secret society, if they answer the question at all.

## 5. Is the statement in the *Encyclopaedia Britannica* true?

Definitely. The article in the *Britannica* is definitely not a piece of anti-Mason propaganda; as a matter of fact, it is just the opposite, written to cast the most favorable light on Masonry. Not surprisingly, the article was written by a dedicated, high-ranking English Mason. So, yes, the statement is trustworthy.

## 6. Then, on what basis do Masons deny being a secret society?

They do so by classic, typically Masonic, double talk. They will usually defend their position by saying, "We are a society with secrets, but not a secret society." This is comparable to saying, "I am a farmer with thousands of cattle, but I am not a cattle farmer."

While they deny being a secret society, they meet behind painted or draped windows and a closed, guarded door, and everything they do there is secret and protected by death oaths. They will admit this but point out that the fact of their existence is not a secret. Therefore, they say, they are not a secret society. It doesn't require a logician or a linguist to determine that this is merely word juggling.

## 7. What do the Masonic authorities say about secrecy?

They are unanimous about the necessity for secrecy and the gravity of any violation of the secrecy. Secrecy has been a hallmark of Masonry since its beginning; it is one of its landmarks, and they take it very seriously.[3]

Albert Mackey, one of Masonry's most authoritative writers, said in his *Textbook of Masonic Jurisprudence*,

> The secrecy of this institution is another and most important landmark. . . . If divested of its secret character, it would lose its identity, and would cease to be Freemasonry. . . . Death of the Order would follow its legalized exposure. Freemasonry, as a secret association, has lived unchanged for centuries; as an open society it would not last for as many years.[4]

## 8. Then, why would Masons want to deny being a secret society?

They seem to be increasingly defensive about Masonry as a whole and are anxious to reassure those outside the

Lodge that they are a fine, virtuous, and benevolent organization. Because of this, they are quick to deny the existence of anything negative in the public's perception of the institution. A secret society must have dark and sinister things to hide (which of course is true); for this reason, they don't like being known as a secret society.

## 9. Are the doors really guarded during their meetings?

Definitely; as a matter of fact, this guarding of the door is one of the "ancient landmarks." The guardian of the door is an officer of the lodge, and his title is "Tiler." The spelling of this word varies, like so much in Freemasonry, but as it is here is the most common. The origin of the word is uncertain, but most Masons, if they have knowledge of it at all, will tell you that the name comes from the fact that an otherwise finished roof must be "tiled" on its ridge, or rain and snow can come through. Thus, a "tiled" lodge is one in which the Worshipful Master can be assured that there is no one in the lodge hall except Masons of the appropriate degree and that none can enter or hear what is being said and done. With this in mind, the Tiler is usually armed, symbolically, with a sword.

## 10. Do Masons have to take an oath of secrecy?

Absolutely. A portion of the bloody and horrible death oaths for each degree is the promise to keep not only the secrets of the order's rituals and lessons but also the secrets of one another's crimes. Over and over, the Mason must swear, on penalty of mutilation and death, to "ever conceal and never reveal" any such secrets.

## 11. If the Masons want to have secrets, what's so wrong with that?

There is nothing at all wrong with secrecy *per se*; there are times when secrecy is the wise and right course. But, here again is that Masonic spirit of exclusiveness and elitism. What makes secrecy so wrong and such a contradiction, in this case, is that Masonry is supposed to have the answers to life, death, and eternity. In this sense, it is hideously wrong to take the position that "We have the secrets to life, death, and eternity, we are the only ones who know these things, and rather than hasten to share these wonderful secrets with all of mankind, we are going to keep most of the world from knowing our wonderful, life-giving secrets, let them wander in darkness, and be damned. We will share these wonderful, all-important secrets with only a few of our friends." As I said before, logically and ethically, this is indefensible.

The Christian imperative, since we really do possess the answers to life, death, and eternity, is to shout it from the house tops and invite the entire human race into our redeeming truth and fellowship. The true gospel is for "whosoever;" the invitation of Jesus is for everyone who is thirsty and wants His unspeakable gift to come and take the water of life freely. And, He has commanded us to spread this good news all over the world. *This* makes sense!

## 12. Do they really have secrets?

No. Most Masons believe that all their "secret work" is unknown outside Masonic circles, and they will fight— literally—to protect their "secrets," but, as in so many other ways, they are deceived.

## 13. How can Masons think their matters are secret if they aren't?

They believe so for the same combination of reasons that they believe that Masonry is Christian, is based on the Bible, and is not a religion. They have been told that no one but a Mason could possibly know anything about Masonry's secrets because none of the "secret work" is in writing. To reinforce this, the Mason must swear that he will never write down any of the "secret work." This, like so much else that Masons are told, is simply untrue; it can all be found, one way or another, in writing. But, they believe that it doesn't exist in writing, and almost none of them will take the time or trouble to investigate, read, and think for himself on the matter.

The truth of the matter is that there is only one well-kept Masonic secret, and that is that there are no Masonic secrets!

## 14. How can these secret things of Masonry be seen and read?

I was amazed to learn how easily most of this material can be obtained. Some of it can simply be found in libraries. Such Masonic books may often be found in used book stores. (Many such stores will have a Masonic section.) I have bought some key Masonic reference books off the shelf in new book stores. (Here, also, they will frequently be found in the "Occult" section.) Some classics may be picked up at yard sales, and many are left behind by relatives when they die. But, the most amazing thing of all for me was the discovery that Masonic publishers will sell these books to anyone! I have ordered many over the years and have never had to tell them whether I am a Mason (nor have I ever been asked!). I have found that at least one Masonic publisher will even sell the books of "secret work" and ritual written by anti-Masonic writers.

For example, there is a published version of the secret recognition test for Shriners (the test a Shriner from a different club, a stranger, must pass in order to be admitted to a meeting). I bought a copy for twenty cents! The most difficult book to obtain is Albert Pike's classic, *Morals and Dogma*. This book is given only to Scottish Rite Masons with the Thirty-second Degree and comes with the requirement that it must be protected from unauthorized eyes, and provision must be made for it to be returned to the Scottish Rite upon death of the owner. (In some places, this requirement is "on penalty of death.") Even this one can be bought when a used copy is available.

Yes, anyone who really wants to can obtain all these "secret" books; yet the average Blue Lodge Mason not only believes that someone like you and I could not possibly have one of these books, he doesn't even believe that they exist!

## 15. How have their secrets come to be known outside the Lodge?

Since about 1826, there have been no Masonic secrets. After the kidnapping and murder of Captain Morgan in 1826 and the posthumous publication of his book (the first exposé of Freemasonry), there was a tidal wave of angry reaction to Masonry.[5] In addition to the revealing of all the Blue Lodge "secret work" in Morgan's book, influential Masons all over the country deliberately went to court and made public all the higher degrees as well. From that time on, a succession of books has been published, plainly revealing all that once was truly secret.

So, since about 1830, it is true that they have no secrets. But, you will have a tough time convincing most Blue Lodge Masons of this fact. (See chapter 17, "Death Oaths and Masonic Execution.")

---

## Endnotes

1. Albert Mackey, *Encyclopedia of Freemasonry*, rev. ed. s.v. "Mysteries, Ancient" (Chicago, New York, London: Masonic History Co., 1927), 497-500.

2. *The New Encyclopaedia Britannica*, 15th ed., s.v. "freemasonry," 302.

3. Landmarks are foundational, indispensable matters of Masonic law, dating, in one form or another, since the first codification of Masonic doctrine in the early eighteenth century. The landmarks (i.e., secrecy, men only, belief in a "Supreme Being," obedience to the Worshipful Master, etc.) are sometimes called "The Unwritten Law of Masonry," as opposed to the Constitutions, which are called "The Written Law of Masonry." There is much reference in Masonic writings to "The Ancient landmarks"; however, as in all of Masonry, there is much confusion and contradiction concerning the landmarks, with varying numbers,

from seven (according to Massachusetts) to fifty-four (according to Kentucky). Henry W. Coil *Encyclopedia of Freemasonry* includes not only various lists of landmarks, but includes twenty-five definitions of the word!

4. Albert Mackey, "23rd Landmark: Secrecy," *Jurisprudence of Freemasonry*, rev. and enlarged ed., Book II (Chicago: Chas T. Powner Co., 1975), 17.

5. William Morgan, *Illustrations of Masonry*, printed for the Proprietor, republished (Batavia, NY: 1827).

# 15

# Masonry and Deception

*Deliver my soul, O LORD, from lying lips and from a deceitful tongue.*

—Psalms 120:2

## 1. Is there deception in Masonry?

Yes there is, from top to bottom. In fact, the more I learn of Freemasonry, the more deception I see in small matters and in large ones.

## 2. What do you mean by that?

The public is completely deceived (at least, that is Masonry's intention and the attempt) as to the basic nature of Masonry, its teachings, and the "secret" things they do. In addition, there is vast and widespread deception of the public in terms of Masonic charities and how the public's money is spent. The worst example of this known to me is the Shrine. (See chapter 5, "The Shrine: Islam in Freemasonry.")

But, worse than this, by far, is the deception by Masonry of its own members.

## 3. In what way are the members of the Lodge deceived?

Freemasonry is, for the vast majority of its members, a lifelong succession of deceptions. Here are a few examples:

• The first deception usually occurs when the member, still only a prospect, is assured that Masonry is not a religion, is based on the Bible, will make him a better man, and, if he is a Christian, that the Lodge will make him a better Christian.

• The initiations are deceptions in that the candidate is not told in advance of the death oaths, let alone their terrible content. The Ku Klux Klan is, in this way, more honorable than the Lodge; for their oath is not a death oath, and the candidate is not only told of the oath in advance, he is required to read it, so there can be no misunderstanding concerning the obligation he is about to undertake.

• The candidate is deceived in that he is told, just before taking his first oath of obligation, that there will be nothing in the oath that would conflict in any way with his personal religious faith. Here he is being lied to when the very taking of the oath is such a violation for a Christian or a religious Jew, forbidden both in the New Testament and the Old. And, this is to say nothing of its unscriptural content, promising to conceal other men's crimes and containing hideous penalties one writer has described as those "of which a common cannibal would be ashamed."[1] (See also chapter 17, "Death Oaths and Masonic Execution.")

• Here, in the administration of the oath, is not only a deception but an enormous flaw in logic which leaps at me, yet it always seems to go unnoticed by those involved. When the Worshipful Master assures the initiate, just before administering the oath, that there will be nothing in the oath that will be in conflict with his personal religious faith, he hasn't asked the initiate what his personal religious faith is!

• The initiate is deceived when led through his oath of obligation as a Master Mason and swears to uphold certain aspects of personal morality. The wording of the oath is extremely deceptive because of its very subtle immoral meaning.

He must swear never to "cheat, wrong or defraud" another Master Mason or a lodge of Master Masons, "I knowing them to be such." Sound good? It isn't. Note that this leaves the Master Mason free to "cheat, wrong or defraud" anyone else in the world, as long as it isn't another Master Mason, and even that will be alright as long as he doesn't know that he is dealing with a Mason.

Likewise, he must swear not to "violate the chastity of a Master Mason's wife, his mother, sister or daughter, I knowing them to be such." Sound honorable? It isn't. This leaves the initiate free to commit fornication or adultery with anyone else's wife, mother, daughter, or sister, or even those of another Master Mason as long as he is not aware of their Masonic connection. And, even a woman with a known Masonic connection is fair game if she has no chastity to violate.

These things are deceptive! These things are wrong!

• The initiate is doubly deceived in the third degree (Master Mason):

(1) First, he is deceived in an emotionally cruel way by being led to believe that the initiation is finished when it is hardly begun. He takes his oath, gets his instruction, goes back to the preparation room, puts his clothes on, is given a "jewel" (badge of office) to wear, and thinks he is a Master Mason. Then, he is taken back into the lodge hall, is rebuked by the Worshipful Master for wearing an "unauthorized jewel," is threatened, and is sent back to the preparation room. There he has to again remove his clothes, is again blindfolded, and is led by the cabletow back into the lodge hall for the traumatic remainder of the ritual.

(2) Second, he is deceived by being led to believe that the legend of Hiram Abiff involved in the second part of his initiation is historical and has no spiritual significance. Actually, the story he must reenact, portraying Hiram, is pure myth; worse than that, it is terribly significant paganism. The unwitting candidate is required to portray Hiram, not having the slightest idea what it is all about, entering

into the death, burial, and resurrection of the Masonic messiah, Hiram Abiff, who is actually Osiris, the Egyptian sex god.

Sound impossible? Unbelievable? Let's allow a few of Masonry's most respected historians to speak for themselves:

> That part of the rite [third degree initiation] which is connected with the legend of the Tyrian Artist [Hiram Abiff] should be studied as a myth and not as a fact. . . . Outside of Masonic tradition there is no proof that an event such as is related in connection with the "Temple Builder" ever transpired and, besides, the ceremony is older by more than a thousand years than the age of Solomon. . . . It is thoroughly Egyptian.[2]

> It [the legend of Hiram Abiff] is thoroughly Egyptian, and is closely allied to the Supreme Rite [third degree] of the Isianic Mysteries [the pagan mystery religion of Isis and Osiris].[3]

> We readily recognize in Hiram Abiff the Osiris of the Egyptians.[4]

> Osiris and the Tyrian Architect (Hiram Abiff) are one and the same.[5]

It couldn't be much plainer than this, could it?

• The initiate is deceived when he is promised that his initiation will bring him from darkness into the light; yet, he never quite gets to the light. From degree to degree he searches for it, and, finally, at the culminating moment in the Scottish Rite, the lecture of the Thirty-second Degree, he is told that the light is "out there somewhere" and that he must go find it on his own.

• The Mason is deceived when his money is taken in dues and initiation fees and accumulated in vast sums by high-level leadership, where it is used for things of which the individual Mason is unaware, and of which most would not approve. Not only is the money used to provide luxurious offices, chauffeur-driven limousines, and memberships in expensive clubs for high-level leaders, but, much worse, it seems true that the power the money represents is ultimately applied to ungodly global political and spiritual matters. (See also chapter 22, "Masonry, the New Age, and the New World Order.")

• The individual Shriner is deceived when he solicits money at intersections for the Shrine's famous charities. He, with rare exception, believes sincerely that every penny of the money he collects in his bucket will go to build and operate those hospitals, when the truth is that as little as two cents out of every dollar will be so used.

• The individual Mason is deceived as to the true nature of Masonry, believing that his degrees and lessons in the Blue Lodge are wholesome, moral, and based on the Bible; he doesn't know that he is participating in the rankest paganism. He doesn't realize, when he is required to kiss the Bible to seal his oath that he is, as former Mason Jim Shaw so eloquently expresses it, "kissing Jesus goodbye at the altar of Baal."[6]

• The individual Mason is deceived when he is taught, subtly and repeatedly, that he can earn his way to heaven by his moral living, good works, and obedience to his oaths.

## 4. Do the local Lodge leaders realize that they are deceiving their members in these ways?

They usually don't. If they would stop to think about what they say and do, as you and I are doing now, they would realize that they were being deceptive. But, for the most part, they are simply reciting the same things they have heard and said, over and over, assuming that they are right and good, themselves victims of this self-perpetuating deception.

## 5. Do the leaders at the very top realize that they are deceiving the rank and file members of Blue Lodge Masonry?

They definitely do realize that they are deceiving Masonry's rank and file, but I must qualify this statement.

There are many of Masonry's high-level leaders, including Grand Masters and other officers at Grand Lodge level, who are themselves so deceived that they, like most officers in the Blue Lodges, believe that what they are doing is right. There is definitely a spiritual blindness that, in time, puts a veil over the minds of Masons so that things which are obvious to those of us on the outside are hidden from them.

## 6. Can you give an example of this?

Yes. Again, I could cite many, but that would be unworkable, and one must suffice. The Reverend Dr. Forrest D. Haggard has for many years been pastor of the Overland Park Christian Church (Disciples of Christ) in Overland Park, Kansas. He is interim general secretary of the World Office of the Churches of Christ (Disciples, Christian and Church of Christ). One year after his ordination in the Church of Christ in 1949, he was made a Master Mason. He has been an ardent Mason ever since, is past Grand Master of the Grand Lodge of Kansas, and has risen to the Thirty-third Degree. He is the author of *The Clergy and the Craft*, a book of the Masonic view of the "harmony" between Masonry and the Church. He is, by anyone's standards, a prominent Masonic leader.

In the spring of 1993, in the midst of the intense conflict within the Southern Baptist Convention over Freemasonry, the *Scottish Rite Journal* published a series of articles by clergymen and others identified with "organized religion," all defending Masonry and declaring its compatibility with being a Christian. In the May issue, the inside front cover is a full color portrait of the Reverend Dr. Haggard, resplendent in his colorful clerical robe, and his is the lead article. His title is "Freemasonry and Religion are Compatible," and the illustration of the article consists of a Christian cross, the crescent and star of Islam, the Star of David of Judaism, and, in the center, the Masonic square and compass. With my first glance at the story, I saw an obvious contradiction! I didn't have to think it over, I didn't have to meditate, ponder, or consult the major reference works. On its face, it was a total refutation of the entire premise of his article! It doesn't require a doctorate in theology to realize that orthodox Christianity, Islam, and Judaism are hopelessly incompatible with one another, absolutely mutually exclusive! And, yet, Haggard, with all his learning and experience, is telling the world that the opposite is true. Any member of a Bible-believing Christian church (or, for that matter, a synagogue or mosque) should know that you can't have Jesus and Mohammed, or Jesus and rabbinical denials of Him, and you certainly can't have Islam and Judaism in the same camp! And, yet, the Reverend Dr. Haggard, with all his education and a lifetime in the pulpit, is saying that you can.

How can this be explained? How can we understand this? There are only two possibilities: either Haggard is a wicked, sinister, devious man, deliberately publishing propaganda intended to deceive and lead good men to everlasting damnation; or he is a sincere, nice guy who thinks that he is doing right—a good man, terribly deceived. I choose to believe the latter and find no reason to doubt it. I see the doctor as a classic example of the self-perpetuating, deadly deception, even among prominent Masonic leaders.

## 7. But, are there also leaders at the top who do know that they are deceiving the rank and file?

Yes, and in this is found the most evil, most despicable, and most outrageous deception in all of Freemasonry's dark repository of lies. Blue Lodge Masons, the multitudes of the rank and file, make the entire Masonic system, with its hierarchy of degrees, orders, and offices, possible. They give the money (an enormous amount when totaled) that makes it all possible, they give their loyalty (which is priceless), they believe in it, defend it, and go to their graves believing that they have been doing something honorable. Nothing could be further from the truth, and, in this, they are deliberately and cynically deceived by those at the pinnacles of Masonic power.

## 8. How are they deceived in this way?

Blue Lodge Masons are deliberately taught false meanings of the symbols in their degrees and lessons.

## 9. But, what is so important about the meanings of the symbols?

In Masonry, as in all occult sciences, symbols are not just important, they are the very essence of the teachings. Masonry describes its teachings as being a system "expressed in symbols and veiled in allegory." At the root, there is a basic love for big words in Masonry (their philosophers, it seems, can always be counted on to say "expectorate" or "masticate" when "spit" or "chew" would suffice); but, in this case, their words are instructive.

Their teachings in Blue Lodge consist primarily of lessons in morality and religion, including the explanation of the meanings of symbols (See chapter 16, "Masonry and Its Symbols."). The meanings presented to the Blue Lodge Mason are, without exception, wholesome and healthy, stressing such things as responsibility, self-control, and fairness in dealing with others. Ah, but what about the part that their teachings are "veiled in allegory"? This means that the elements and words are symbolic, go to another level for more meaning, and are only suggested or hinted at by the teachings. The true meanings, in other words, are something else, something hidden, something other than what they are being taught.

## 10. But, what is so wrong with that; maybe the leaders just want the members to learn to think?

No, that's not all there is to it. The truth is much more sinister, much more evil, much more outrageously wrong. To fully grasp the significance of this, it is necessary to know that the temple of Solomon is the central symbol of

Blue Lodge Masonry, ultimately representing Freemasonry's wisdom and knowledge. The portico (porch) of the temple was the outermost part, a place where the common people could go; the really important things took place on the inside. And, remember that the Masonic plan of salvation requires one to be enlightened, which means to gain the knowledge of the meanings of the symbols.

In his classic Masonic reference work, *Morals and Dogma*, Albert Pike, Supreme Pontiff of Universal Freemasonry, Sovereign Grand Commander of the Supreme Council of the Thirty-third Degree, Mother Council of the World, etc., that preeminent Masonic authority, makes the following, amazing statement:

> Masonry, like all the religions, all the mysteries, Hermeticism and Alchemy, *conceals* [emphasis his] its secrets from all except the Adepts and Sages, or the Elect, and uses false explanations and misinterpretations of its symbols to mislead those who only deserve to be misled; to conceal the Truth, which it calls Light, from them, and to draw them away from it.[7]

Does this sound outrageous? Unbelievable? It is. But, wait, it gets still worse. Pike goes on:

> The Blue Degrees are but the outer court or portico of the Temple. Part of the symbols are displayed there to the initiate, but he is intentionally misled by false interpretations. It is not intended that he shall understand them; but it is intended that he shall imagine he understands them. Their true explication [explanation, meaning] is reserved for the Adepts, the Princes of Masonry. It is well enough for the mass of those called Masons, to imagine that all is contained in the Blue Degrees; and whoso attempts to undeceive them will labor in vain, and without any true reward violate his obligations as an Adept.[8]

If words have any meaning (and they do), this is the

most outrageously wrong statement in all my knowledge of Masonry. Here this quintessential Masonic elitist is saying that the peasant masses of the Blue Lodge Masons are inside Masonry (the temple), but just barely (restricted to the common people's porch). This far, it is classic elitist snobbery, but not wickedness. But, then, he goes on to say that only a portion of the symbols the Mason must understand are shown to him, not all, though he thinks he has them all (this is worse). Then, he says, very plainly, that the Blue Lodge masses are deliberately taught false meanings. This is outrageous! This means that the occult adepts, the aristocracy of Masonry who believe that a true understanding of Masonry's symbols is required for enlightenment and acceptance in the "Celestial Lodge on High where the Great Architect of the Universe presides," deliberately withhold some of the symbols from the rank-and-file Masons and, much worse, condemn them to darkness by deliberately teaching them false meanings of the ones they do have!

I can't imagine anything more immoral! It is like teaching a gullible, trusting man that he can swim by merely wiggling his ears, adding that he must not move his arms or legs, and, then, dropping him in the ocean, miles from shore, with his hands and feet tied. The Masonic form of deception is worse, however, for it is an eternal dip in the sea. And, forever is a long time to be wrong.

Incidentally, Pike was prophetic in saying that those who might try to "undeceive" the peasantry of Masonry "will labor in vain." It has been my experience that most Masons, when presented with the truth about Freemasonry, even this statement by Pike, refuse to hear it. They just take offense, close their minds, and go on trying to learn to swim with their ears.

---

## Endnotes

1. Martin L. Wagner, *Freemasonry, an Interpretation*, republished, (Grosse Pointe, MI: Seminar Tapes and Books, 1912), 556.

2. Daniel Sickles, *Ahiman Rhezon and Freemason's Guide* (New York: MaCoy Publishing Co., 1911), 195.

3. Albert Mackey, *Lexicon of Freemasonry* (Charleston, SC: Walker and James, 1852), 195.

4. A.T.C. Pierson, *Traditions of Freemasonry* (New York: Anderson and Co., 1865), 240.

5. Sickles, *Ahiman Rhezon*, 236.

6. You can read Jim's story in the Huntington House book, *The Deadly Deception*, by Shaw and McKenney.

7. Albert Pike, *Morals and Dogma*, rev. ed. (Washington, DC: House of the Temple, 1950), 104, 105.

8. Ibid., 819.

# 16

## Masonry and Its Symbols

*A wise man will hear, and will increase learning... to understand a proverb, and the interpretation; the words of the wise, and their dark sayings.*

—Proverbs 1:5-6

### 1. What is the meaning of the Masonic symbol commonly seen on men's lapels, rings, autos, etc.?

Before I can answer that question, one thing must be made very clear: all Masonic symbols have two meanings. There is the outer, obvious meaning, which Masonry calls the "exoteric" meaning, and there is the inner, hidden meaning, which Masonry calls the "esoteric" meaning. As in all of Masonic symbolism, the true meaning is the hidden, esoteric one. Once again, we witness that spirit of elitism that runs through all of Masonry, seeing the Masonic rank and file as unenlightened, gullible, "vulgar" (common) masses compared to the elite, knowledgeable, wise "adepts."

Hear the words of Albert Pike:

> The symbols of the wise are the idols of the vulgar, or else as meaningless as the hieroglyphics of Egypt to the nomadic Arabs. There must always be a common-place interpretation for the mass of initiates, of the symbols that are [by comparison] eloquent to the Adepts.[1]

When you ask about the Masonic symbol, you probably mean the familiar square and compass, with the *G* in the center. This is undoubtedly the most familiar Masonic symbol. Like all the other Masonic symbols, this one has both an esoteric and an exoteric meaning; to make things a little simpler, let's call them the apparent meaning and the true meaning.

## 2. What is the apparent meaning of the symbol?

It is the combination of the square, which teaches Masons to "be square" in all their dealings, especially with other Masons, and the compass, which teaches Masons to "circumscribe their passions," meaning to exercise self-control.

## 3. And, what is the meaning of the letter *G*?

Here is an excellent example of Masonic contradiction, yet one which seems to go unchallenged by Masons. In the first degree, the initiate is told that the *G* represents deity, that is God. But, in the second degree, he is assured that it represents geometry, "the first and noblest of science," by means of which the secrets of the universe may be discovered.

This was the only thing concerning Masonry which my father ever said to me, and he didn't bring it up. I once asked him what the *G* meant, and he answered simply, "God." This single word was the only word he ever spoke to me, or to anyone in my presence, about Masonry. And, for my father to lie was unthinkable; he was the most honest, honorable man I ever knew.

## 4. If these are the outer meanings, then what are the true, inner meanings?

At this point, in order to answer your question, we must plunge directly into the murky heart of the matter of Masonic symbolism, and, I promise you, it will be heavy going.

Since the true meaning of Freemasonry lies in its being descended from, and a revival of, the mystery religions of ancient Egypt, especially the worship of Isis and Osiris, the true meanings of its symbols are sexual. Shocking as this may be, I suppose that we shouldn't be surprised since the cult of Isis and Osiris was a fertility (i.e., sex) cult. In plain language, those pagans worshipped sex and reproductive power ("fecundity").

The sun, worshipped by nearly all pagan groups, represented life-giving sexual reproductive power, the active, male, generative force, with its rays penetrating the passive, female earth, causing new life to come forth. The personified image of the sun, usually worshipped in such fertility cults, was (and is) the phallus, the male reproductive organ, and their "worship" services were often orgies. It was to just such a scene that Moses returned when he came down off Mount Sinai after forty days with God. That golden calf wasn't just a sweet little baby cow, it was a bull calf with prominent horns and conspicuous genital equipment. It was the personification of dominant male strength and reproductive power commonly worshipped in the fertility cults of the East.

Realizing these foundational facts, sickening though they be, the rest of the answers about Masonic symbols will make more sense to you, once your head ceases to spin.

## 5. Then, what about that basic Masonic symbol, the square, compass, and *G*?

According to Masonry's top authorities, the symbol represents sexual reproduction. The Compass represents the dominant, active, male "reproductive principle." The square, inverted, represents the passive, receptive, female "reproductive principle," and the relative positions, the one above and the other beneath, is no accident. The combination, thus arranged, represents the sun penetrating and impregnating the earth to bring forth new life. The Compass also represents loftier, spiritual functions, while the Square represents the more earthly, carnal, and base functions.

In the Entered Apprentice symbol, the points of the Compass are usually beneath the Square; in the Fellowcraft symbol, one point is usually above and one below; in the Master Mason symbol, both points of the Compass are usually above the Square, symbolizing complete dominance.[2]

It doesn't take much thought to see that not only are the Square and Compass symbols of the ancient worship of nature and sex, but that the female is in the decidedly inferior status.

## 6. Then, what about the letter *G* in the center; what is its true meaning?

The true meaning of the *G* is that of the phallus, the representation of deity in the Egyptian fertility cults.[3] In the legend of Osiris and Isis, Osiris was murdered and his body was cut into fourteen pieces and thrown into the Nile. Isis found and recovered all parts but one, the phallus, which had been eaten by a fish. So, she made an image of the phallus of Osiris, put it in the temple, and caused it to be worshipped as the image of the slain sun god. That's how it was supposed to have happened back in ancient Egypt, and Masonry has taken the legend, the symbolism, and the worship for its own.

Albert Pike explained that the *G* in English-speaking Lodges actually represents a corruption of the Hebrew letter *yod*. "The mysterious YOD of the Kabalah" is the "image of the Kabalistic Phallus."[4]

Who would ever have thought that this pagan phallic worship would be brought into our midst, right into wholesome, "Christian," Hometown, USA, and practiced by some of its finest citizens? I assure you that it was shocking news to me (and is also shocking news to most Masons!). That golden *G* that hangs on the wall above the head of the Worshipful Master in the East is a symbol of deity alright, but it is not the God of Abraham, Isaac, and Jacob.

## 7. And, are you saying that Masonic philosophers admit these things and even put them in writing?

Absolutely. In fact, there is so much of this material existing in mainstream Masonic literature that most serious students of Masonry will never read it all. And, 99 percent of all Masons will never read any of it.

## 8. Then, why don't all Blue Lodge Masons know these things?

Because, in the first place, they are taught the outer, wholesome meanings, and they believe them. Their minds are made up. After that, they never learn the true meanings because they don't read the materials for themselves. If they would find the source books and read them, they would know; but they almost never do.

## 9. Do you mean that these incredible things are true and that the Masons acting all this out don't know the true meaning of what they are doing?

Blue Lodge Masons, the heart and backbone of American Freemasonry, representing 95 to 97 percent of all American Masons, are deliberately deceived as to the true meaning of their own symbols. That's right. They are deliberately deceived about the true meaning of the symbols, as we have seen already. (See chapter 15, "Masonry and Deception.") The vast majority of Masons, even dedicated ones, never go beyond the Blue Lodge, are never exposed to the true meanings, and go to their graves believing the lies. Even those who do go on into the higher degrees, where the occult, pagan nature of Masonry is much more apparent, seldom pay attention or think about it enough to realize the contradictions between Blue Lodge teachings and the truth. Their minds are already made up before they go into the higher degrees, and most of them really don't care about the lesson content; they just want to get the degrees, get it over with, join the Shrine, and get on with the parties and good works. All Thirty-second Degree Masons are given a copy of Albert Pike's *Morals and Dogma* (or its equivalent), but the vast majority never open it.

## 10. But, why would the elite leaders at the top of the system want to deceive the rank and file in the Blue Lodge in this way?

I believe that the answer to this perplexing question is that the leaders know that if the rank and file knew the truth about the true nature of Masonry and the real meaning of the symbols, they would not only leave Masonry immediately, they would wish they had never joined it in the first place, which may compel them to dissuade others considering joining. I have never seen this explained in Masonic doctrinal writings or even dealt with as a matter of speculation, but this seems to me to be the only reasonable answer, and, on this point, I have never been challenged.

## 11. What other Masonic symbols are there in the Blue Lodge?

There are many, way too many to deal with here. They all have occult meanings about which the Blue Lodge Mason is never told. Besides the square and compass and the *G*, among the most important of these are the point within the circle, the right triangle (the forty-seventh problem of Euclid), and the all-seeing eye.

Let me explain briefly the outer (false) meaning and the inner (true) meaning and cite Masonic authorities for each.

*Point within a Circle.* The Blue Lodge teaching is that the point represents the individual Mason, and the circle represents the limitations of his duties. In other words, he can't do just whatever he wants, he must be responsible and faithful to his responsibilities. The two parallel lines flanking the circle are supposed to represent "the Holy Saints John," in whose names the Blue Lodge is always opened. The true meaning is, of course, occult and sexual.

The point represents the phallus, the circle represents the vagina, and the juxtaposition of the one within the other represents sexual union.[5] The two parallel lines are actually the zodiacal signs of Cancer and Capricorn, where the sun is found during the summer and winter solstices, respectively. They were depicted by the ancient Egyptians as two rigid snakes, heads at the top. You think I must be making this up? Well, let's hear from the Masonic authorities:

Albert Mackey:

> Phallus, a representation of the virile member, which was venerated as a religious symbol . . . . It was one of the modifications of Sun worship, and was a symbol of the fecundating power of that luminary. The Masonic point within a circle is undoubtedly of phallic origin. . . . It is derived from Sun-worship, and is in reality of phallic origin.[6]

> The point within a circle is an interesting and important symbol in Freemasonry, but it has been debased in the interpretation of it in the modern lectures (the wholesome teachings in the Blue Lodge) and the sooner that interpretation is forgotten by the Masonic student the better it will be. The symbol is really a beautiful but somewhat abstruse allusion to the old Sun-worship, and introduces us for the first time to that modification of it known among the ancient as the worship of the phallus.[7]

> They are said to represent St. John the Baptist and St. John the Evangelist; but they really refer to the solstitial points Cancer and Capricorn in the Zodiac.[8]

Albert Pike:

> These two Divinities, the Active and Passive principles of the Universe, were commonly symbolized by the generative parts of man and woman . . . the phallus and cteis [vagina], emblems of generation and production, and which, as such, appeared in

the Mysteries. The Indian Lingam was the union of both, as were the boat and mast, and the point within a circle.[9]

The Solstices, Cancer and Capricorn, the two Gates of Heaven are the two pillars of Hercules, beyond which he, the Sun, never journeyed; and they still appear in our lodges, as the two great columns, Jachin and Boaz, and also as the two parallel lines that bound the circle, with a point in the center.[10]

**The Triangle.** The usual, outer interpretation of the equilateral triangle in Masonic teaching is that of the Triune God. The hidden, true meaning is, again, pagan and sexual. With the base line down and the point up, it represents the male reproductive element, the phallus. With the base line up, it represents the female reproductive element, the vagina. When the two are combined to form the six-pointed star, they represent sexual union. Recalling that the square, with the point down, symbolizes the female principle, it is interesting and significant to realize that this square, with a line drawn across its upturned arms, becomes the inverted triangle, also symbolic of the female principle. Additionally, the compass above, with its points connected by a line, becomes the male principle, in union with the female.

The equilateral triangle, a basic symbol of deity, is subtly present in the Blue Lodge in that the Master, Senior Warden, and Junior Warden, the three officers whom Blue Lodge Masons must obey, are arranged in a triangle, and the candles around the altar, representing the sun, moon, and Worshipful Master, three representations of deity, are arranged in a triangle. Again, let's hear from the authorities:

Albert Mackey:

In the higher degrees of Masonry, the triangle is the most important of all symbols. . . . Among the Egyptians it was a symbol of universal nature, or the protection of the world by the male and female energies of creation [sexual power].[11]

Writing of the combination of two triangles, the one base up and other base down, Mackey further explains, "The interlacing triangles or deltas symbolize the union of the two principles or forces, the active and the passive, male and female. . . ."[12]

J.D. Buck:

> Back of this trilateral glyph [triangle, representing the Hindu fertility god trinity, Brahma, Siva and Vishnu] AUM, lies the philosophy of the secret doctrine. . . . Each deity in this triad was regarded as masculine, and as having his sakto or female consort which was represented by the triangle with its base upward, and is the symbol of the door through which every human being comes into the world.[13]

Albert Pike:

> . . . the Triangle, to all Ancient Sages the expressive symbol of the Deity . . . Osiris and Isis, Har-oeri, the master of light and Life, the Creative Word.[14]

***The Right Triangle.*** The right triangle, one containing a ninety degree angle, is an important symbol in Blue Lodge Masonry. It is illustrated in monitors and other Masonic sourcebooks with a rectangle drawn on each of its three sides, depicting what Masons call "the 47th problem of Euclid" (the theorem of Pythagoras). The meaning of the symbol taught in Blue Lodge is that Pythagoras was "initiated into several orders of priesthood, raised to the sublime degree of a Master Mason" during his travels through Asia, Africa, and Europe, and that during his sojourn in Egypt he discovered the relationship between the square of the hypotenuse and the other two sides, shouted "Eureka!," and sacrificed one hundred oxen (which Masonry, always in search of a bigger word, calls "a hecatomb"). The lesson of the "right-angle triangle," according to the Blue Lodge, is that a Mason is "to be a general lover of the arts and sciences."[15]

Ah, but let's hear what the authorities really say:

Albert Pike:

> . . . the 47th problem of Euclid, a symbol of Blue
> Masonry, entirely out of place there, and its mean-
> ing unknown (to the Blue Lodge Mason) . . . The
> perpendicular is the Male, the Base the Female; the
> Hypotenuse the (sexual) product of the two.[16]

> The 47th Proposition is older than Pythagoras.
> [Things are never ancient enough to suit Masonic
> philosophers!] We must suppose that the perpen-
> dicular is designed by them to represent the mas-
> culine nature, the base the feminine, and that the
> hypotenuse is to be looked upon as the offspring of
> both; and accordingly the first of them will aptly
> enough represent Osiris, or the prime cause; the
> second Isis, or the receptive capacity; the last, Horus,
> or the common effect of the other two.[17]

Albert Mackey:

> Among the Egyptians it was the symbol of universal
> nature; the base representing Osiris, or the male
> principle; the perpendicular, Isis, or the female
> principle; and the hypotenuse, Horus, their son, or
> the product of the male and female principle.[18]

**The All-Seeing Eye.** Ask any Mason what the eye within
a triangle represents, and he will tell you that it represents
the eye of God, seeing all, knowing all, and watching over
us (or, he will say that he can't talk about it). And, he will
be sincere, for this is what he has been taught, and he
believes it to be true. Ah, but here again, this is only the
"exoteric" meaning and not the true meaning. The true
meaning of this symbol is with Osiris, the Egyptian sun
and sex god, the actual object of worship in the Masonic
Lodge. Let's again hear from the Masonic authorities:
Albert Pike:

> The Blazing Star has been regarded as the emblem
> of Omniscience [all-knowing], or the All-seeing Eye,
> which to the Egyptian initiates was the emblem of
> Osiris, the Creator.[19]

Albert Mackey:

> It is a very ancient symbol, and is supposed by some to be a relic of the primitive sun-worship. . . . An important symbol of the Supreme Being, borrowed by the Freemasons from the nations of antiquity . . . the Egyptians represented Osiris, their chief deity by the symbol of an open eye, and placed this hieroglyphic of him in all their temples.[20]

## 12. But, do all these symbols and their meanings really matter; aren't they just a very minor part of Masonry?

In Masonry, symbols not only matter, it could be said the symbols are everything, that symbols, in a sense, *are* Masonry. Symbols are the language of Masonry, and their meanings are its lessons. The old English lecturers and their American descendants define Freemasonry as "a system of morality, expressed by symbols and veiled in allegory."[21] And, Albert Mackey agrees that allegory and symbolism are the only things in Masonic teachings that really matter:

> All the legends of Freemasonry are more or less allegorical, and whatever truth there may be in some of them in an historical point of view, it is only as allegories, or legendary symbols, that they are important.[22]

## Endnotes

1. Albert Pike, *Morals and Dogma,* rev. ed. (Washington, DC: House of the Temple, 1950), 819.

2. Ibid., 11, 850, 851.

3. Ibid., 15, 771, 772.

4. Ibid., 5, 757, 758, 771, 772.

5. There does seem to be something universal about this imagery. I can remember little boys demonstrating it with their fingers in a Kentucky school yard to impress the other little boys, and I can remember seeing, from a docking troopship, Japanese prostitutes doing exactly the same thing on a pier during the Korean War, advertising their trade.

6. Albert Mackey, *Symbolism of Freemasonry* (Chicago: Chas T. Powner Co., 1975), 352, 353.

7. Albert Mackey, *The Masonic Ritualist* (New York: MaCoy Publishing Co., 1903), 62.

8. Mackey, *Symbolism*, 352.

9. Pike, *Morals and Dogma*, 401.

10. Ibid., 506.

11. Mackey, *Symbolism*, 195, 361.

12. Albert Mackey, *Encyclopedia of Freemasonry*, rev. ed. s.v. "Triangle" (Chicago, New York, London: The Masonic History Co., 1927), 801.

13. J.D. Buck, *Mystic Masonry* (Chicago: Chas T. Powner Co., 1925), 62.

14. Pike, *Morals and Dogma*, 861.

15. Mackey, *The Masonic Ritualist*, 129, 130; Henry Pirtle, *The Kentucky Monitor* (Louisville, KY: Standard Printing Co., 1921), 148,149.

16. Pike, *Morals and Dogma*, 789.

17. Ibid., 86-88.

18. Mackey, *Encyclopedia*, 800.

19. Pike, *Morals and Dogma*, 15, 16.

20. Mackey, *Encyclopedia*, 47, 48.

21. Ibid., 47.

22. Mackey, *Symbolism*, 315.

# 17

# Death Oaths and Masonic Execution

*But above all things, my brethren, swear not, neither by Heaven, neither by Earth, neither by any other oath; but let your yea be yea, and your nay nay, lest ye fall into condemnation.*
—James 5:12

## 1. Do Masons have to take blood oaths in order to join?

Yes, they definitely do. With the possible exception of an extremely important man who is made a Mason "at sight," it is not possible to become a Mason otherwise.[1]

## 2. Are these oaths also called "death oaths?"

Yes, the terms "blood oath" and "death oath" are synonymous. Although some may use the term "blood oath" to mean a ceremony where two people cut themselves in order to bleed and then mix their blood, becoming "blood brothers," that is not what is meant here. When I use the expression "blood oath" in relation to Freemasonry, I mean that the penalty for breaking the oath is bloodshed and death. For this reason, "death oath" is a better term, and the one I normally use.

I must make it clear, however, that these are not Masonic terms. The Masonic term for the oath of a degree or order is "oath of obligation."

## 3. Does a man take only one oath to become a Mason?

Oh, no. There is one death oath for each degree, plus one for the Shrine and any other "side" order or degree a man might seek. This means that a Master Mason (third degree Mason) has taken three such death oaths. A Thirty-second Degree Mason has taken at least thirty-two such oaths. Mr. Evans Crary, who wrote the foreword, was a Thirty-third Degree Mason, a York Rite Mason (Knight Templar), and a Shriner. When he turned away from Freemasonry to follow Jesus, he violated forty-four death oaths!

## 4. What is the nature of the oaths?

They are basically similar. Like everything else in Masonic ritual, they are very formal, wordy, and pompous, and each one involves some form of torture, mutilation, and death. In each oath, the initiate swears that he will not violate the secrecy of the degree, swears to certain peculiarities to the specific degree, and agrees that if he should violate his oath, especially the secrecy provision, he will allow himself to be tortured, mutilated, and put to death, always in horrible ways. One Christian writer expresses it well when he refers to their "horrid oaths and penalties of which a common cannibal would be ashamed."[2] It is interesting to me that even the oath of the Ku Klux Klan is not a bloody, death oath. (Some of the oaths are in Appendix B at the back of the book.)

## 5. What is the purpose of these oaths?

The purpose of the oaths is to bind the initiate to the organization, to separate him from the outside world, and like any oath, to require him to take seriously the commitment he is making. Such declarations are almost as old as man; promises of any kind are considered to be binding even though they may subsequently be broken.

But, in Masonry, there is an added, unhealthy, unscriptural aspect: fear. The oath of obligation is designed to instill fear in the initiate, to bind him even more tightly to the organization and to his promises with cruel cords of fear.

## 6. Do the oaths actually put the man in fear for his life?

Definitely, and this is especially true at first. After a man has taken the first oath (Entered Apprentice Degree), he is better prepared for subsequent degrees and their oaths aren't so much of a shock; but, in each of the Blue degrees, the candidate is deliberately made to feel helpless and kept disoriented and confused, and, with each oath, there is real fear. After a man has already taken ten or fifteen such oaths, the impact is lost, partly because he is not blindfolded and roughed up but also because repetition has taken the edge off their wording.

## 7. Can this have a lasting effect on the man who takes these oaths?

Definitely! I believe they are designed to do just that. Whether or not the originators of Freemasonry had this in mind, it is nevertheless true (and at least Satan had it in mind). These oaths (and other parts of the ritual) are a powerful means of mind control, and the men are extremely vulnerable when they take them. At first, they are made vulnerable by disorientation and fear. In the higher degrees, they are just as vulnerable to the occult, pagan poison in the oaths because of pride and deception. Their minds are open to suggestion and programming because they see themselves "moving up" and are proud of it, and there is openness to the lectures of the degrees because this is what they have sought. At the very first, they were vulnerable because of confusion, disorientation, and fear; later on, they are still vulnerable because of openness.

There can be, and often is, a powerful form of mind control accomplished (or at least set in motion) in the death oaths.

## 8. How do Masons, especially Christians, justify these terrible oaths?

They can't. There is no way to justify this affront to God, the violation of Scripture, and what it does to the men who take these oaths. Until recently, however, they were seldom called upon to defend them because most people didn't know about them.

In the 1830s and thereafter, there was widespread public knowledge, at least among Christians, of the oaths and other negatives concerning Masonry. But, in time, that public awareness dissipated like morning fog, and, until the recent reawakening of the church to the realities of Masonry, hardly anyone outside the Lodge was aware of the oaths.

Now, when Masons are asked how they can justify the oaths, some will deny that they have taken any (You see, one of the things wrong with the oaths is that the men must promise to lie if necessary.), for that admission would itself be a violation of their oaths. Some will answer that they "can't talk about such things." The rest will say that they took the oaths but didn't mean them literally, that they were "just symbolic."

To those who would say, "I didn't take seriously all that stuff about the mutilation and death, I really didn't mean it," I say that you should have meant it; you should have taken it seriously because you sealed that oath with the words "So help me God, and keep me steadfast in the performance of same." It is a dangerous, sinful thing to "vow a vow" in God's name, call upon Him to make you able to perform it completely, and not mean it.

Some Masons try to explain the oaths away by saying, "Oh, the oaths aren't important in Masonry, they're just part of the ritual and really don't matter." They should remember the question in Blue Lodge ritual, part of the test an initiate must pass. The question is "What makes you a Mason?" The only correct answer is "My obligation." So, according to the Lodge, the oath not only matters, it is what makes a man a Mason! The same question and answer are also part of the higher degrees.

## 9. Who would carry out these executions that the oaths call for?

This is one of the most important questions that could be asked about these oaths, yet hardly anyone ever asks. People, including Masons, apparently don't think it through, but this is a terribly important point! The answer is, obviously, that other Masons must do it.

And, that leads us to something of extreme importance that remains undiscussed (no one has ever pointed it out to me), and I believe that not one Mason in one hundred thousand ever realizes it. In taking these oaths, the Mason is also agreeing that he will torture, mutilate, and murder any other Mason who violates the oaths! He is promising to become a Masonic torturer and executioner, if need be. After all, who else would do it? Who, but other Masons acquainted with the man and his behavior, would even know that it should be done, let alone have any reason to do it? No one! Think about this—especially if you are a Mason. There is no other possibility.

## 10. Has this ever happened? Have men ever actually been murdered for violating their Masonic oaths?

Yes, it has really happened. The first known Masonic execution in the United States took place in 1826 in New York. It may have happened before, in the 109 years since that first Grand Lodge was organized in England, but the first one on record in this country was in 1826.[3]

## 11. Who was the victim, and how did it happen?

The murdered Mason was one Captain William Morgan of Batavia, New York, a veteran of the War of 1812, a Christian, and a Mason of thirty years. Masonic versions of the story differ, of course, most of them denying any Masonic guilt, even denying that Morgan was ever a Mason, implying that he was motivated by his having applied for acceptance in a lodge and being rejected.[4] But, when one assembles all versions and all available evidence, the following story emerges.

Captain Morgan, a Mason for thirty years, became convicted about the immorality of Masonry, especially for a Christian. He wrestled with the question. (It is never easy to renounce instantly something one has accepted, embraced, and served sincerely.) He finally decided that he must not only leave Masonry, but that he should write a book exposing it to the public. After he had written the book, but before it was published, both he and his publisher, Col. David C. Miller, were kidnapped by Masons. Morgan was taken to Fort Niagara, New York, and held captive for three days in a powder magazine (Today, we would call it an ammunition bunker.) while Masonic authorities debated what to do with him. It was decided that he must die; lots were drawn to choose the killers, and three men drew the lots. He was taken out into the Niagara River, bound, and weighted. He begged for his life to be spared, for the sake of his young wife and small children, but he was thrown into the river and drowned.

## 12. Did this become known right away?

Yes, it became known almost immediately. His publisher, Colonel Miller, escaped and initiated a search for Morgan, but he was not found. (His body was found and identified a year later.)[5] DeWitt Clinton, governor of New York, offered rewards for his recovery and the capture of the perpetrators. When there was still no body, a groundswell of angry reaction began to rise, and, within months, the book was published. This triggered a series of other such renunciations by prominent Masons, and there grew a tidal wave of angry public reaction which nearly swept Freemasonry off the American scene. More than 90 percent of all American Masons left the Lodge in anger, and the vast majority of American Lodges closed. Many Grand Lodges ceased to meet; the Grand Lodge of Massachusetts turned in its charter.[6] Numerous books, tracts, and sermons were written condemning Masonry for what it is. Prominent men of all Masonic orders and degrees deliberately went to court and saw to it that all the degrees, all the secrets, all the rituals were read into the court records and so became public knowledge. Since that time, there have been no Masonic secrets, except for the details of the Thirty-third Degree initiation, which have been revealed in the Huntington House book, *The Deadly Deception.*

There was even an anti-Mason (political) party organized, with its members winning many political offices. In 1832, this party even ran a slate for president of the United States and carried one state (Vermont), this in spite of the fact that their candidate, William Wirt, was a Mason who had supposedly seceded. It was determined later that he hadn't and may have been planted by the Lodge in order to sabotage his own election. In 1836, William Henry Harrison ran for president as an anti-Mason and lost; he ran again in 1840 (as a Whig) and was elected. Many prominent political leaders (including President Millard Filmore) began their careers in the anti-Mason party. It was no small thing.

## 13. Was anyone ever convicted of the abduction and murder of Morgan?

Yes, several men were convicted of kidnapping, assault and battery, and false imprisonment. But, no one was ever convicted of the murder, although two of the three made confessions late in life. Henry L. Valance, the man who actually pushed Morgan in the river, confessed to his physician on his deathbed.

## 14. Have there been any such Masonic executions since Captain Morgan?

Yes, but only God knows how many. Charles Finney, evangelist of the nineteenth century, himself a seceding Mason and author of an excellent exposé of Freemasonry, said that he could document more than twenty Masonic executions since Morgan. As recently as 1982, there appears to have been a Masonic execution that made the news. A man was found dead, hanging from Blackfriars Bridge in London, England. He was Roberto Calvi, member of the internationally powerful "P2" Lodge in Rome (the members of this lodge call themselves "Black Friars") and an international banker with strong ties to the Vatican. The story made a brief initial splash in the news and disappeared. According to close associates, Calvi was about to reveal incriminating things about powerful men, all members of the P2 Lodge. The inquest declared the circumstances of his death "open" (meaning that it could be murder rather than suicide). Masonic symbolism associated with the death pointed to European Masonry, and even the London police (most of them Masons themselves) theorized that it looked like a Masonic execution. The name of the bridge from which his body, drugged before his death, was hanged is a further indication of this.

## 15. Could such a Masonic execution happen here in this day?

Yes, but I hasten to add that most American Masons wouldn't be part of such a thing. The vast majority of Masons are definitely not murderers; they are good men. But, the fact that such things have happened and can still happen is a powerful indictment of the Masonic system which lies to them, takes their money, makes merchandise of their loyalty, and uses them.

Today, Masonic execution is most conceivable among the elite, globalist, international leadership (which includes, incidentally, the P2 Lodge of Rome). It is interesting to me that Masonic execution is also conceivable at the opposite end of the Masonic spectrum, in some rural areas where the world view is extremely limited, where only Blue Lodge Masonry is known, and where they take it very seriously.

What an irony, and how eloquent an illustration of the system, that execution is most likely among the cynical, arrogant, sophisticated, patrician elitists and among the passionate, plebeian, unsophisticated zealots—the calculating manipulators and the manipulated patriots who believe whatever they say. This point is worthy of contemplation.

---

## Endnotes

1. Being made a Mason "at sight" is an unusual event, explained in chapter 11.

2. Martin Wagner, *Freemasonry, an Interpretation*, republished (Grosse Pointe, MI: Seminar Tapes and Books, 1912), 556.

3. There is reason to suspect (and there are many who believe) that Mozart, a Mason who died very young, was poisoned for revealing Masonic secrets in his piece *The Magic Flute*.

4. Masons, in an attempt to discredit me, accuse me of the same thing. The fact is that I have never applied for acceptance by a lodge of any kind, including Freemasonry.

5. Although the body was somewhat decomposed, it had been significantly preserved by having been weighted and submerged under the cold water. The coroner's jury declared unanimously that it was that of Captain Morgan.

6. Henry W. Coil, *Masonic Encyclopedia* (New York: MaCoy Publishing Co., 1961), 57, 58.

Freemasonry's influence in Mt. Liberty Baptist Church of Murphy, North Carolina, is apparent from the stained glass windows. This one is the Masonic symbol for the "All-seeing Eye" (the eye of Osiris).

# 18

## Masonry, Presidents, and the Founding Fathers

*Thou shalt provide out of all the people able men, such as fear God, men of truth, hating covetousness, and place such over them. . . .*

—Exodus 18:21

### 1. Is it true that all U.S. presidents have been Masons?

No, this is definitely not true. It is very common for Blue Lodge Masons to say this when trying to justify Masonry, and most of them probably believe it. It is just another example of the tendency of people to accept favorable generalizations; it is comforting and requires no individual effort or thought. The truth is that Masonic presidents of the United States are a distinct minority, and presidents who were devoted Masons a tiny, almost non-existent minority.

### 2. Then, how many U.S. presidents have been Masons?

Here, again, we have a problem in trying to nail down facts concerning things Masonic; it isn't always easy to know what it means to "be a Mason."

Ronald Reagan is not a Mason, although he was made

an honorary one in his office at the White House during
his second term. But, he has never been inside a lodge hall
and wouldn't know what to do if he went. Not even
Masonry's top leaders consider him to be a Mason. He
isn't.

And, then there is the interesting case of Lyndon
Johnson. He took the first degree as an Entered Apprentice and never went back. As a completely pragmatic politician, it appears that Lyndon "got his card punched" so
he would have Masonic support in politics and then left it
all behind. This was most unusual! It is almost never done!
A spokesman at the House of the Temple in Washington,
D.C., headquarters of the Supreme Council of the Thirty-
third Degree, Southern Jurisdiction, spoke of this as he
showed me through the museum.[1] There was a large,
decorative portrayal of American presidents who have been
Masons, and it included Lyndon Johnson. He said that
Johnson really shouldn't be counted as a Masonic presi-
dent because of his having never gone beyond the Entered
Apprentice degree. And, he isn't counted; in the book,
*Masons Who Helped Shape Our Nation*, published by the
Supreme Council of the Thirty-third Degree, Southern
Jurisdiction, there is an illustration of Masonic presidents,
and Johnson is not included.

## 3. Then, how many U.S. presidents are counted; how many have actually been initiated fully into the Masonic lodge?

There have been fourteen. Fourteen out of forty-two
presidents have been Masons.[2] Even among these fourteen, several seem questionable. James Monroe received
only the Entered Apprentice degree in 1775 and never
proceeded beyond it through the Blue Lodge; his reasons
are unknown.

William Howard Taft was made a Mason "at sight"
(which means that he was not initiated, a dispensation
usually reserved for "important" people) in 1901 and appears not to have been active in any way, being a "member
at large" of the Grand Lodge of Ohio.[3]

Warren G. Harding, another extremely pragmatic politician, received only the first degree in 1901 and didn't receive any other degrees until after he became president in 1921. After becoming president, he was quickly made a member of the Royal Arch and the Scottish Rite and was made a Knight Templar, all in 1921.

## 4. Have any U.S. presidents been serious Masons?

Yes, a few have been what I would call serious Masons. Andrew Jackson, although records are less than conclusive, is recorded as having been Grand Master of Tennessee. Gerald Ford certainly embraced Masonry; he is Thirty-third Degree in the Scottish Rite and is a member of the Shrine.

But, the true Masonic president of them all was Harry Truman. He was a passionately devoted Mason and came up through the system, all the way from Entered Apprentice to being Grand Master of Missouri, before he was either vice-president or president. He was recognized as a Master Ritualist (one who excelled in memorizing and directing the rituals) and Thirty-third Degree. He never joined the Shrine. When president, he frequented the House of the Temple at lunchtime to play the piano there, and sometimes this could interfere with business. On at least one occasion, it was necessary for a messenger to go to him and say, "Mr. President, would you please stop playing, or use the damper pedal; the Master is trying to open the Lodge [open a meeting of the Lodge there]."

## 5. But, what about the Founding Fathers of the nation; weren't they all Masons?

Definitely not; here, again, is a commonly believed generalization that is simply not true. Ask any ordinary rank-and-file Mason, and he will probably tell you that all of them were Masons; and he will probably be sincere. But, the truth is that while some of the Founding Fathers were Masons, many were not.

The books and pamphlets published by Masonic sources would give one the impression that all those men in Philadelphia were running around in Masonic aprons, giving one another grips and passwords, laying Masonic cornerstones all over town, that the Constitutional Convention "met on the level and parted on the square," and that they opened and closed Lodge every time the Continental Congress met!

Such was simply not the case, Scottish Rite paintings and publications to the contrary notwithstanding.

## 6. Who are some of the Founding Fathers who actually were Masons?

The most prominent—and the one Masons will always hold up to "prove" that Masonry is good—is George Washington. Besides Washington, other prominent men who were Masons included Benjamin Franklin (who was also a Rosicrucian) and John Hancock, famed first signer of the Declaration of Independence. Franklin was a zealous Mason and one of the first members of the Philadelphia Lodge. Hancock was taken into an English lodge while visiting in Canada and later affiliated with a lodge in Boston. Although not in the category of "Founding Father," Paul Revere is a prominent man in American history; he was definitely a Mason and became Grand Master of Massachusetts.

*But, they never mention Benedict Arnold.* Masonic historians and propagandists, in painting their pictures and writing their stories of the Masonic Founding Fathers, never mention one of the most famous ones. Benedict Arnold, whose name became a synonym for "traitor," was a Mason and remained one for life.

## 7. What about Thomas Jefferson, Alexander Hamilton, John Adams, James Madison, Thomas Paine, John Jay, and the other Founding Fathers; weren't they all Masons?

No, they definitely were not, not a single one. In fact, not only these men, but most of the other Founding Fathers you may be able to think of, were not Masons.

Contrary to popular Masonic opinion, and some of what I can only call Masonic propaganda, Jefferson was never a Mason. John Jay was never a Mason. Thomas Paine was not only not a Mason but wrote an essay in which he traced the origins of Freemasonry to ancient paganism, specifically to the Druids.

John Adams, Washington's vice-president and second president of the United States, was not only not a Mason, but was opposed to Masonry. His son, John Quincy Adams, although one cannot validly call him a Founding Father, grew up in the colonies, was a young man during the revolution, was sixth president, and certainly played a role in shaping the nation. John Quincy Adams was a passionate anti-Mason.

Daniel Webster felt that the Masonic oaths of obligation should be against the law: "In my opinion, the imposition of such obligation as Freemasonry requires should be prohibited by law."[4]

John Marshall, the "Great Chief Justice," is one of those whom Masonry holds high as an example of Masons who made our nation. Like Washington, he became aware of the Masonic myths being spread abroad while he still lived. Before his death in 1835, he repudiated the practices of Masonry falsely attributed to him and stated that he had been in a lodge only once in the past forty years. He wrote, "The institution of Masonry ought to be abandoned, as one capable of producing much evil, and incapable of producing any good which might be affected by open means."[5]

## 8. But, how could George Washington have been a part of it; was he just not as pure as we have been taught?

Here was, for me, the most troubling thing in all of Masonry as I began to learn the truth about it, for he has always been a hero to me.

Washington is definitely their number one icon; when the rightness of Masonry is questioned, the very first thing most Masons will do is to tell you that Washington was a Mason. They continuously hold him up before the world as their great representative. That huge ziggurat (my term) that they have built just inside the capitol beltway in Alexandria, Virginia, towering over the countryside, is named for him (the George Washington Masonic National Memorial). The first thing with which the visitor is confronted upon entering this building is a huge inscription of a letter written by Washington, carved into the stone wall. Every lodge hall of any means has a portrait of Washington, wearing his Master's jewel and sash, and that same portrait frowns from the opening pages of most Masonic *Monitors*. Paintings of Washington in his Masonic apron and Master's jewel, wielding a trowel at cornerstone ceremonies, adorn much of Masonic literature, especially public relations materials.

The more I learned the ugly truth about Masonry, the more troubled I was with Washington's apparently being such an important part of it. So, I began to research Washington's Masonic history, and the more I learned of the truth about it, the more relieved I became. And, I can now say, the truth has not been told—not nearly. Yes, Washington was "as pure as we have been taught"; he was human, to be sure, but he was an honest, admirable, extremely honorable, Christian man of prayer.

## 9. Then, how can we explain his having been a Mason, especially such an active, prominent Mason?

The first thing we need to know is that he wasn't "such an active, prominent Mason." Those paintings of Washington in his Masonic regalia, which practically all Masons believe were painted from life, are spurious. Ask any honest historian (including honest Masonic historians), and he will tell you that Washington never sat (or "stood") for any such portrait. Every painting of Washington from life is known by collectors and curators; and the last one, undoubtedly the most famous, was never finished. Those paintings on lodge walls and in Masonic *Monitors* are apocryphal, painted after Washington's death.

Even while he still lived, there was growing impetus among Masons to canonize Washington and capitalize on his place "in the hearts of his countrymen." The Masonic myth of Washington's commitment to Freemasonry was growing, and Washington, nobody's dummy, perceived this and was troubled by it. It troubled him enough that he took pains to try to clarify the situation and set the record straight before he died.

He failed, but the fact that he tried is significant, and what little evidence survives is enough to establish that the generally accepted Masonic version of Washington's Masonic connection is so vastly overblown as to be simply untrue.

## 10. Well, was he, or was he not, a Mason?

As much as I wish it weren't true, the fact is that Washington was a Mason of the third degree, a Master Mason.

## 11. Then, doesn't that mean that he was not as pure as we have believed, that he was a part of all that is wrong with the unscriptural, Christ-denying Masonic system?

No, it definitely does not.

## 12. How can you deny these things when you admit that he was a Mason?

Let me explain. First, I will summarize, and then I will be more specific.

As a young man, George Washington joined "an English Lodge" in Fredericksburg, Virginia.[6] He apparently soon became inactive. We don't know the reason for this; it may simply have been that he was away so much, surveying boundaries in the wilderness and fighting England's battles with the French and Indians. But, whatever the reasons, he apparently soon became inactive and was never active again.

One foundational fact is much more important for

purposes of our inquiries than is the extent of his zeal, or lack of zeal, for Masonry. That fact is that the institution of Masonry young George Washington joined in 1752, and which survived until fourteen years after his death in 1799, acknowledged and honored Jesus Christ as the Savior of lost mankind and offered prayers in His name. It was not until the formation of the United Grand Lodge of England in 1813 that Jesus was downgraded to the status of merely one of the exemplars and prayers became "universal," making no mention of Him. Washington was dead fourteen years before American Masonry took on this Christ-denying character.

But, you may ask, wasn't the Masonry Washington joined still rooted in paganism? Yes, as much as I would like to deny it, the answer is *Yes*. But, it was still a very different Masonry from that of Albert Mackey, Albert Pike, Joseph Fort Newton, Daniel Sickles, J.D. Buck, and Manly Palmer Hall—as different as night and day.[7]

## 13. Did Washington ever renounce Freemasonry?

What scanty evidence there is concerning this question indicates a "yes and no" answer. There is no conclusive evidence that he completely renounced Masonry before he died; however, it is clear that he was at least ambivalent about Masonry, even the "Christian" Masonry that he knew. He took the trouble to correct, when he could, the growing Masonic myth about him. He wrote to a friend, correcting the record, indicating that he was troubled over the stories "of my Presiding over the English Lodges in this country." He said that he presided over none and that he had not even been inside a lodge hall "more than once or twice within the last thirty years," quite a different story from that of the Masonic myth.[8] In addition, Washington, before his death, warned the nation to beware of secret societies.[9] He didn't mention Masonry specifically, but neither did he specifically exclude it.

Was Washington a dedicated, Bible-believing Christian? Yes. Was he an active, zealous Mason? No. Was he "founding master" of a lodge in Alexandria?[10] No, nor was he ever Master of any other lodge. Had he attended lodge since his induction as a young man? No, he had not even "been in one, more than once or twice in over thirty years" when he died. But, did he ever renounce Masonry completely? There is no evidence that he ever did, although it is reasonable to assume that had he lived to see the changes and the murder of Morgan as John Marshall did, he would have joined Marshall in renouncing Masonry completely.

## 14. What about the other Founding Fathers who actually were Masons; did they belong to the same, Jesus-confessing Masonry as Washington?

Yes, they certainly did. And, this, I believe, casts an entirely different light on Masonry's claims on the Founding Fathers.

## Endnotes

1. I want to be on record as saying that I have been treated very graciously when I have visited the House of the Temple, as I have been when dealing with them by phone or mail.

2. This is as of this first publication in 1994.

3. See chapter 9, "Masonry's Membership: How Men Join."

4. W.J. McCormick, *Christ, the Christian and Freemasonry* (Belfast, Ireland: Great Joy Publications, 1984), 112.

5. Ibid., 111,112.

6. That is what such a lodge was called in early American history, because they were chartered by the Grand Lodge of England; a "Scottish Lodge" was one chartered by the Grand Lodge of Scotland.

7. Many a Mason over the years, including prominent leaders, has clung to his belief in the Bible as the inspired Word of God and in Jesus as unique Savior. All Masons didn't instantly abandon Jesus and His Word as of the day in 1813 when the Grand

Lodges of England united. For example, even that zealous and influential Mason, Rob Morris, founder of the Order of the Eastern Star, while Grand Master of Kentucky, suspended a lodge Master for saying that the Bible was "a good sort of history, but not sacred." Morris was later overruled, and the suspended Master restored; but, this is an eloquent illustration of the lack of unity, and theological complexities, involved in Masonry, especially in the first, formative century.

8. Letter from Washington to Reverend G. W. Snyder, dated 25 September 1798.

9. Finney, Charles G., "The Character, Claims and Practical Workings of Freemasonry" (Southern District of Ohio: Western Tract and Book Society, 1869), 222.

# 19

## Masonry and Divided Loyalties

*No man can serve two masters: for either he will hate the one, and love the other; or else he will hold to the one, and despise the other.*

—Matthew 6:24

### 1. Is there any conflict between a Mason's oaths of loyalty to the Lodge and his other commitments of loyalty?

Yes, and this conflict is one of the most insidious things about Freemasonry. By taking his oaths of obligation, the Mason puts himself in the position of swearing to put his loyalty to the Lodge above other commitments of loyalty.

### 2. How then can the Mason justify this?

He can't. If he thinks about it, he finds himself in the position of having to violate one commitment or the other; whatever he does, it will be wrong.

### 3. What do you mean by that?

Let me answer with an example. If a Mason has sworn to conceal the secrets of all brother Masons and is subsequently called as a witness in a trial in which another

Mason is accused of a crime of which the first Mason has knowledge, what does he do? He is sworn in court to tell the truth, "So help me God"; yet, he is already sworn, in the Lodge, to conceal the man's secrets, including crimes, and he swore, "So help me God" there also. What can he do? He must violate one solemn oath or the other. If he lies in court, he violates his oath as a witness (and, incidentally, is guilty of perjury); if he tells the truth, he violates his Masonic oath.

This is definitely a problem of divided loyalty.

## 4. Do Masons actually swear to conceal the crimes of other Masons?

Absolutely. They cannot become Masons any other way. It is his oaths of obligation that make him a Mason, and his oaths include such swearing, both in the Blue Lodge and in the higher degrees.

## 5. Just what kind of vows do they make about concealing other men's crimes?

In the Master Mason degree (third degree), the climactic degree of the Blue Lodge, the candidate must swear to conceal the secrets of a brother Master Mason, "murder and treason excepted." This, of course, binds the Master Mason to conceal all other wrongdoing, including rape, mayhem, stealing, etc. In some places, the words "and this left to my own discretion" are added, thus making it "honorable" to perjure concerning, or to otherwise conceal, even murder and treason.

In the higher degrees, such as the seventh (Royal Arch) degree, he swears the same oath but adds the words, "without exceptions."

## 6. Do these men really mean these things?

They should, for they swear, "So help me God, and keep me steadfast in the performance of the same." But, to answer your question directly, I would say that many really mean them, while many are really just going through the motions. But, even those who don't mean them must have lingering thoughts that trouble them. They certainly should.

## 7. Can this become a problem in the courts?

Yes, obviously, and here is one of the most ominous aspects to Freemasonry's long arm. If a man is accused of a crime, and a witness called against him is a Mason, this witness is obviously on the horns of a divided loyalty dilemma. He must either perjure himself for the accused, or tell the truth and violate his Masonic oath.

If even one member of the jury is a Mason, he is obliged to "go to the relief" of the accused. If the accused gives the Masonic sign of distress, the jurist is obliged to vote for acquittal and, at the least, hang the jury.

## 8. What is this sign of distress?

This signal is called the "Grand Hailing Sign of Distress." It is supposed to be given only when a Mason believes his life is in danger (as it well could be in some court trials) and consists of standing, raising the arms above the head, lowering them to the sides in a certain way, and saying, "Oh Lord my God, is there no help for the widow's son?"[1] I should also point out that the accused doesn't have to interrupt court by standing up to shout this out; it can be conveyed in subtle ways.

## 9. When this distress sign is given, what is another Mason supposed to do?

He is supposed to help the man, so long as there is a better chance of saving the distressed man's life than of losing his own. Here is an obvious flaw in Masonic selflessness but still a real problem in a court case.

## 10. Are there any judges who are Masons?

Definitely, and here is the gravest problem of divided loyalties. The Masonic judge has sworn on a Bible (or on some "holy book") to lie if necessary in order to protect other Masons. Yet, he has also sworn on a Bible to uphold and defend the Constitution and to render fair and impartial judgment of all who come before him accused. What does such a Masonic judge do when the accused standing before him is another Mason? Here is an impossible case of divided loyalty, and its implications go to the very heart of our system of law and justice.

## 11. Does this ever happen?

Yes, it is bound to happen. In spite of Masonry's claims to exalted morality, Masons do wrong things all the time, like the rest of us, and sometimes they get caught. Even if such a situation occurs only rarely, it is still a problem. Even if the judge, prosecutor, defense counsel, or witness tells the truth and does the honest thing, the problem of divided loyalty still exists.

## 12. What happens in such a case?

There are many possibilities, all the way from a Masonic policeman who decides not to write him up, through a prosecutor who decides not to prosecute, an investigator who "loses" evidence, to a judge who renders biased judgment, or a governor who grants unjust clemency.

And, all these things have happened at one time or another.

## 13. Has it happened recently?

Such events must be everyday affairs in this country with overloaded police departments and courts and with thousands of crimes committed every hour. Most, of course, go undiscovered or unreported. Of those reported, most don't make the news. However, there was a case in New York state a few years ago that seems a valid example. A Mason, director of a boys camp for the Order of DeMolay, was accused of sexually abusing a number of the boys under his care. The parents filed criminal charges. When the case was finally tried, the defense counsel, the prosecutor, and the judge were all Masons. The charges were reduced to a relatively meaningless misdemeanor, and the camp director walked away with a gentle slap on the hand. The parents of the boys appealed, and I don't know whether or not it has yet been resolved.

Another case that made the news in recent years took place in Cincinnati, Ohio. A man, a Mason, accused of installing an illegal wiretap, testified that he subsequently went to a superior who was also a Mason and asked him to get the charge dropped or reduced. During the conversation, the accused man showed his Masonic ring and asked, "Is there no help for the widow's son?" The charge was reduced.[2]

## 14. Do these Masonic vows produce divided loyalties in other areas of life?

Yes, and the possibilities are almost endless. Officers and noncommissioned officers in the armed forces are supposed to perform their duties fairly and impartially and are sworn to uphold and defend the Constitution against all enemies, foreign or domestic. Many of the men are Masons, and some of the women belong to the Eastern Star or some other adoptive Masonic group. Can they live up to their commitments as military leaders and to their Masonic vows of favoritism at the same time? No. It is not possible, and this is a growing morale and discipline problem of enormous potential.

## 15. Do all Masons take vows that produce divided loyalties?

Definitely. Beginning with the very first degree, each oath binds the man more tightly to the Masonic system and separates him still more from the rest of the world. In fact, in some of the higher degrees, a man swears allegiance to his order or rite above all other commitments, bar none. Think of the implications of that!

Even in the Blue Lodge, doctrinally, the man is required to obey the Worshipful Master and the wardens, and, in some jurisdictions, this applies "no matter what."

## 16. Can it be a problem within the home?

Absolutely, and this is probably the most serious area in which commitments to Masonry can separate and undermine relationships. The moment a Mason takes his first oath of obligation, he is separated from his wife, in very real ways, for life. Not only has he become bonded by death oath to something of which she can never be a part, but she has become "profane," and if she asks him certain questions about what he does in the Lodge, he must lie.[3] Divided loyalties? Yes, serious ones, where there should be none, and they have no remedy except for him to leave the Lodge.

## Endnotes

1. Like so much in Masonry, the details of this sign vary from one place to another, but this sign is everywhere considered to be one of Masonry's most important "secrets."

2. Associated Press, "Masonic Loyalties enter testimony in wiretap trial," *Cambridge, Ohio Daily, Jeffersonian* (8 December 1989): 5.

3. To get an idea of what it means to be classified as "profane," read 1 Timothy 1:9, 10.

# 20

# Masonry and the Occult

*When thou art come into the land which the LORD thy God giveth thee, thou shalt not learn to do after the abominations of those nations. There shall not be found among you any one that maketh his son or his daughter to pass through the fire, or that useth divination, or an observer of times, or an enchanter, or a witch, or a charmer, or a consulter with familiar spirits, or a wizard, or a necromancer. For all that do these things are an abomination unto the LORD.*
—Deuteronomy 18:9-12

*The secret [hidden] things belong unto the LORD thy God.*
—Deuteronomy 29:29

## 1. Does Freemasonry have anything to do with the occult?

Yes, in fact, one might fairly say that Freemasonry is the occult. Many of Masonry's leading men have been occultists, and Masonry is often defined as an occult science. But, let me hasten to explain; I can say this on the basis that virtually every kind of occult activity is carried on among Masons with no rebuke from the hierarchy, and the occult philosophy runs through the entire system.

*173*

## 2. What do you mean when you say that the occult philosophy runs all through Freemasonry?

First, we must be sure that we understand the terms. It is clear to me that the occult permeates Masonry, from top to bottom; but, for you to understand me, we must first define the word *occult*.

## 3. Then, what does *occult* mean?

The word *occult* is derived from the Latin words *occultus* meaning "secret" and *occulere* meaning "to conceal or hide." The word *occult* then, refers to things hidden or concealed. It covers an enormous amount of murky, dark, sinful, and destructive things, but it basically has to do with the seeking of hidden things, such as secret knowledge and understanding not had by most people.

## 4. What's wrong with seeking knowledge?

Nothing is wrong with seeking knowledge; it is not only right and reasonable, it is scriptural. God gave us the ability to think and learn and wants us to use it. What is wrong with seeking knowledge within the occult is two-fold: the means used are wrong, and the purpose is usually wrong.

## 5. What do you mean by that? Why does it matter how and why we seek knowledge?

In occult things, the means are often supernatural avenues, forbidden by God, so the "how" of it matters very much. What also makes the occult so wrong is the "why" of it. The occult is all about power—not the power of God, but power possessed and exercised by the person, by tapping into and controlling the power of (demon) spirits.

## 6. But, some people get involved in the occult in order to help others. How could this be wrong?

Because wrong is wrong. Although people sometimes dabble in the occult for unselfish reasons, it is still wrong, a thing forbidden by God (incidentally, for our own good).

Satan may grant certain knowledge or supernatural powers to those who seek him, but he always exacts a very high price.

## 7. Then, what are these occult things that God forbids?

As I said, there are so many things included under the generic term "occult" that a definition is difficult. It can be summed up, perhaps, as a seeking after hidden things, especially secret or hidden knowledge and the power it bestows. However, God is nowhere in it; it resides completely in Satan's dark and deadly realm.

## 8. What are some examples of occult activities?

Examples of the occult include all forms of divination (seeking hidden knowledge), such as fortune telling, astrology, psychic phenomena, spiritism (consultation with spirits for information and power), magic, witchcraft, and charming.

A useful way to keep it straight is to remember that anything supernatural not done in Jesus' name, or which does not glorify Jesus, is done with Satan's power and is therefore wrong. There are only two sources of supernatural power and experience: the Holy Spirit of God and evil spirits. The Holy Spirit will only glorify Jesus, never anyone else. People with occult satanic powers glorify themselves, Satan, or both.

## 9. But, what does all that have to do with  Masonry?

You might say that it has everything to do with Masonry. You see, in Christian circles, "occult" is a negative word representing sin of the worst kind, an abomination to God. But, in Masonry, "occult" is a positive word, one that denotes favor. The favor which the occult enjoys in Masonry is an outgrowth of the basic nature of Masonry as an occult philosophy and the elitism of Masonry, which values things possessed only by a select few. Keep that always in mind.

Masonry, according to the claims and teachings of
many of its authorities, is an occult science. This is a valid
claim because all of Masonry is a search for enlightenment, a seeking for the knowledge that will purify and
redeem the seeker and give him access to the power of God.

## 10. Do any leading Masons admit being involved in the occult?

Definitely; among Masonry's most authoritative teachers and writers of doctrine are occultists of international
reputation. Until his death a few years ago, Manly Palmer
Hall was one of the leading occult teachers in the world.
He is also a man of whom Masonry is very proud, the
author of *Lost Keys of Freemasonry* and other influential
Masonic books.

## 11. But, what, specifically, is it that ties Masonry to the occult?

Masonry defines itself as a search for "light." This
means enlightenment, the acquisition of knowledge that
redeems and empowers. And, typical of the occult world,
one is to go on searching (through many lifetimes, actually, by means of reincarnation) and, yet, never really find
the light. You see, the occult has no absolutes; one must
go on seeking and seeking. In the occult world, based on
evolution of man and his gradual perfection by his own
efforts, fulfillment is in the seeking, not the finding. This
search for the secret knowledge goes on and on, as the
individual becomes gradually perfected, redeeming himself.

At risk of being repetitious, I must point out that God
and His gracious provision for our redemption through
Jesus are nowhere in all this seeking. It is all something we
must do for ourselves.

## 12. Then, what is this knowledge they seek that is so important?

First, they seek knowledge that supposedly once was
possessed by men in some past age when things were

supposed to have been much better. Somehow, this knowledge was lost (they usually blame it on the Christians and Jews), and now things are crummy. So, there is this endless quest to rediscover that knowledge and wisdom, a "treasure" they usually call "the hidden wisdom of the ancients."

They often think the keys to this lost wisdom are to be found in little green people in flying saucers, buried beneath the sea in Atlantis, somewhere in the mountains of Tibet, or in the mind of some witch doctor worshiping bats in a Mexican cave. Such are places I would never think to look for anything useful, but occultists seem irresistibly drawn to them.

So, in the occult world, the endless search goes on for "the lost and hidden wisdom of the ancients."

## 13. What is the other knowledge that occultists seek?

Second, and much more important, they seek the "lost" knowledge of "the ineffable name." This exalted Masonic language really just means that they want to know the name of God. And, this search, which is at the very heart of Masonry's occultism and the subject of its most important legends and symbols, is the essence of witchcraft, man's rebellion against God.

## 14. What do you mean? What does God's name have to do with witchcraft?

It is a basic principle of occultism, in general, and witchcraft, in particular, that if one can learn the name of a spirit, one can have that spirit's power. So, if knowing the true name of a minor evil spirit can give you that spirit's power, think what it would mean (to the occult mind, at least) to possess the knowledge of the true name of God! You would have God's power! You could be "like the most High" and maybe even bump God and take His place in the universe. As you probably know, this stupid idea is what caused all of Satan's interpersonal problems with God.

So, there you have it. This is serious stuff—and the heart of all the occult search for "lost" knowledge and the power it brings. They believe that the "lost word," the "ineffable name" of God, was known to the priesthood of the pagan mystery religions back in those ancient "good old days," but Christians, Jews, and other narrow-minded bigots stoned or burned all the magicians who knew it, so it was lost. Things have been downhill for mankind ever since, so their story goes, and the search for it by the occultists goes on.

## 15. You surely don't mean that people who go see a fortune teller, call the psychic hotline, or play with a ouija board are trying to obtain God's power!

Of course, I don't mean that. But, all who even dabble in such apparently harmless occult matters are entering the same dark world of the occult, forbidden by God. And, incidentally, such "harmless" dabbling isn't harmless; it can be deadly. Many a dedicated occultist began his dark career with the "harmless fun" of a visit to a palmist or astrologer, seeking hidden (occult) knowledge.

## 16. But, how do you know that Masonry is so involved in the occult?

I assure you that it is no secret. Anyone who cares to inquire will know this. Masonry's authorities are unanimous in the belief that Masonry is a search for that "light," that lost wisdom, that beauty and perfection of the ancient priesthood and its religious system, the mysteries of Isis, Osiris, Mithras, Ashtoreth, and Baal. Their books, lectures, and degrees are full of it.

If I quoted 1 percent of it here, it would be too much for me to write and too much for you to read. But, I will include a few and rest my case.

Albert Pike:

> Though Masonry is identical with the ancient Mysteries, it is so only in this qualified sense: that it

presents but an imperfect image of their brilliancy, the ruins only of their grandeur. . . .[1]

The Occult Science of the Ancient Magi was concealed under the shadows of the Ancient Mysteries . . . and it is found enveloped in enigmas . . . in the rites of the Highest Masonry.[2]

J.D. Buck:

There is a Grand Science known as Magic, and every real Master [Mason] is a Magician. Feared by the ignorant, and ridiculed by the "learned" the Divine Science and its Masters have, nevertheless, existed in all ages. . . . Masonry in its deeper meaning and recondite mysteries constitutes and possesses this Science, and all genuine initiation consists in an orderly unfolding of the natural powers of the neophyte, so that he shall become the very thing he desires to possess. In seeking Magic, he finally becomes the *Majus*.[3]

The tradition of the Master's Word, of the power which its possession gives to the Master [Mason]; the story of its loss and the search for its recovery; the tradition of the Ineffable Name . . .[4]

The Freemason is . . . the nearest to the Ancient Wisdom. . . . He may dig deeper and find not only the Keystone of the Arch, the Ark of the Covenant, the Scroll of the Law, but, using the spirit concealed in the wings of the Cherubim, he may rise . . . and, meeting Alohim face to face, learn also to say "I am that I am!"[5]

But this is the Ineffable Name, which every Master [Mason] is to possess *and become* [emphasis mine].[6]

Joseph Fort Newton:

The three really great rituals of the human race are the Prajapati ritual of ancient Hinduism, the Mass of the Christian Church, and the Third Degree of Masonry. . . . they testify to the profoundist insight of the human soul—that God becomes man that man may become God.[7]

Manly P. Hall:

When the Mason learns that the key . . . is the proper application of the dynamo of living power, he has learned the mystery of his Craft. The seething energies of Lucifer are in his hand.[8]

I rest my case.

## Endnotes

1. Albert Pike, *Morals and Dogma*, rev. ed. (Washington, DC: House of the Temple, 1950), 23.

2. Ibid., 839. It can be revealing to see what words people capitalize; the capitals are in the originals.

3. J.D. Buck, *Mystic Masonry*, 3rd ed. (Chicago: Chas T. Powner Co., 1925), 34.

4. Ibid., 132, 133.

5. Ibid., 45.

6. Ibid., 62.

7. Joseph Fort Newton, author of *The Builders* and *The Religion of Freemasonry* quoted in Henry Pirtle, *The Kentucky Monitor* (Louisville, KY: Standard Printing Co., 1921): xx.

8. Manly P. Hall, *The Lost Keys of Freemasonry* (Richmond, VA: MaCoy Publishing Co., 1976), 48.

# 21

# Masonry and Mormonism

*Even so every good tree bringeth forth good fruit; but a corrupt tree bringeth forth evil fruit.*

—Matthew 7:17

## 1. Does Mormonism have anything to do with Masonry?

Yes, it does. As a matter of fact, Mormonism cannot be separated from Masonry.

## 2. Why do you say that Mormonism can't be separated from Masonry?

Mormonism is, in many ways, a doctrinal sprout that grew from the stem of Masonry. In their rituals and terminology, there are many similarities.

## 3. How are Mormonism and Masonry similar?

They are similar in terms of being secretive about their internal affairs, and both are cultic in many ways.

## 4. What do you mean, that both are cultic? Are you saying that both Mormonism and Masonry are cults?

I didn't say that, but it is probably true. Mormonism certainly qualifies as a cult by almost anyone's definition, and many students of cults classify Masonry as one also. At the very least, both are what I call cultic.

## 5. What do you mean by the word "cultic"?

By cultic, I mean that they have at least some characteristics of cults; both Mormonism and Masonry have at least some cultic traits.

## 6. What are the traits considered to be cultic?

Characteristics considered by most observers to be cultic include secrecy; exclusion of outsiders from the fellowship of the group; complete commitment to an essential doctrine; possession of a secret doctrine, secret rituals and practices from which the public is excluded; blind obedience to a leader (or leaders); the belief that only that group has the truth; the belief that to leave the group will bring destruction of some kind, especially eternal damnation; and shunning, or outright persecution by the group, of any person who leaves. There are others, but these make the point clear.

## 7. Is Masonry a cult?

Most students of cults classify Masonry as a cult. As a matter of fact, Jack Harris, a former York Rite Mason and past Master of his Blue Lodge, wrote a book on Masonry from the Christian point of view, and he titled his book *Freemasonry: the Invisible Cult in Our Midst.*

## 8. Is Mormonism a cult?

There seems to be unanimous agreement that Mormonism is a cult (except, of course, among Mormons). On most authorities' lists of cultic traits, Mormonism would score 100 percent.

## 9. But, except for the fact that both Masonry and Mormonism have some characteristics of cults, what do they have to do with one another?

When Mormonism was in its first, formative years, Joseph Smith, Mormonism's founder and first "prophet," and his brother Hyrum both became Masons. It seems that they became Masons in a somewhat unorthodox way

(Joseph took all three Blue Lodge Degrees in one day!); nevertheless, they did it and learned the Blue Lodge rituals.[1]

## 10. So Joseph Smith and his brother Hyrum became Masons; is that all that makes Masonry and Mormonism "inseparable"?

Oh, no. There is much more. It was not long after Joseph Smith became a Master Mason that he got the "revelation" for the secret temple ceremony. The rituals of the Mormon Temple are so similar to those of Blue Lodge Masonry that there can be no doubt that Joseph lifted most of it directly from the rituals of the Lodge.

## 11. What is it about the two rituals that are the same?

Many things are alike, but a few examples will suffice. Elements apparently stolen by Joseph Smith include the presentation and wearing of an apron, whispering of "secret" information "on the five points of fellowship" (i.e., "foot to foot, knee to knee, breast to breast, hand to back, mouth to ear"), similarities in the oaths of obligation, the penalties and penalty signs for each, and the symbolism of the square and compass, which must be embroidered in significant places on their "magic" underwear.[2]

## 12. Are these similarities in ritual and symbols all that tie Mormonism to Masonry?

No. Not only were both Joseph and Hyrum Smith Masons, but so was Brigham Young, Smith's successor. As a matter of fact, the first five presidents of the Mormon church (its first five "living prophets") were Masons.

## 13. Is Masonry strong in Mormonism today?

No, at least it is not on the surface. As a matter of fact, for a long time the Mormon hierarchy has forbidden Mormon men to become Masons.

## 14. Why have the Mormon leaders not wanted their men to be Masons?

Because of the secrecy that prevails in Mormonism, it is difficult to know. It appears that they feared the divided loyalty that would almost certainly result.

## 15. What about the leaders themselves? Are any of them Masons?

There has been ongoing "talk" to the effect that, while forbidding Masonry to their rank-and-file members, the top Mormon leaders have not only been allowed to join the Lodge, but that it has been required. The persistent rumor has it that those selected for the highest levels of Mormon leadership have been taken out of their home areas, been secretly taken into the lodge, and then returned home. I believe this, but, obviously, it would be almost impossible to document.

## 16. What if a man who is already a Mason wants to join the Mormon church? What happens then?

Until recently, such a man had to resign from the Masonic Lodge. Now, however, this requirement has been dropped. A Mason can join the Mormon church and go right on being a Mason; so, it appears that Mormon men could now join the Masonic Lodge. The bonds between Masonry and Mormonism seem to be growing ever tighter.

## 17. But, back to Joseph Smith; didn't the Masons have something to do with his death?

Yes, and that is an extremely interesting part of his story. Joseph Smith, with his brother Hyrum, died in a blazing gun battle while they were being held in jail. According to most accounts, when Joseph saw that he had no chance, he gave the "Grand Hailing Sign of Distress," lifting his hands above his head and crying out, "Oh Lord, my God, is there no help for the widow's son?" Apparently there was none, for he was immediately shot down. It is also interesting that part of those in the crowd shooting at Joseph and Hyrum were their "brother" Masons.

## 18. So, is that the story of Mormonism's ties with Masonry?

Yes it is, except for one fascinating thought. Joseph Smith joined the Masonic Lodge in 1842 at the very peak of public knowledge and awareness of the wrong things concerning Masonry. When almost everyone knew about Masonry, especially the things wrong with it, when the rest of the nation was leaving the Lodge and rising up against it, Joseph rushed, eyes wide open, to embrace and join it! This, I believe, says a great deal about the character of Joseph Smith, as well as that of his brother Hyrum.

---

### Endnotes

1. Joseph and Hyrum not only became Masons, but, almost immediately, there was trouble. Because of the Mormon practice of polygamy, most Grand Lodges took a stand against admitting Mormons, so the charter for Joseph's lodge was withdrawn. This didn't stop him, though; he just got busy and organized his own, chartering them himself. The ensuing conflicts over Mormons in Masonry lasted many years, and, in a sense, continue to this day.

2. Not all Mormons are initiated into the Temple rites. Those who are initiated are given "magic" underwear, which must be worn next to the skin, night and day, to protect the wearer from harm. It would certainly appear that in the case of Joseph and Hyrum Smith, it didn't work.

# 22

# Masonry, the New Age, and the New World Order

*If therefore the light that is in thee be darkness, how great is that darkness!*

—Matthew 6:23

## 1. Does Masonry have anything to do with the New Age?

Yes, like Mormonism, the New Age and Masonry are definitely interrelated. As a matter of fact, they seem, to me, to be inseparable.

## 2. How, then, is Masonry related to the New Age?

First, I suppose, it is necessary to again define some terms. "New Age" is about as difficult to define precisely as "the occult." We are bombarded today with New Age propaganda, news items (sometimes it isn't easy to tell these two apart!), reports, and advertisements. We all have some awareness of it, but, if asked to define it, we would find it difficult to know how to answer.

Perhaps, for our purposes, the best way to think of the New Age is as a philosophical and religious system that had its modern beginnings at least a century ago. It is basically occult and esoteric (Yes, those terms also describe Masonry), featuring a great deal of spiritism (e.g., contact with familiar spirits, automatic writing, spirit guides, etc.). It is a "feel good" movement, denying such unpleasant matters as sin, judgment, and hell. It recognizes a coming "messiah" whom they call Lord Maitrayah (variously spelled, but pronounced "Mah-tray-ah") who soon will come to earth from "somewhere out there" to usher in the "New Age" (hence the name) of Aquarius, an indefinite period of peace, good will, prosperity, and all-round happiness.[1]

Sounds too good to be true, doesn't it? Well, it is.

## 3. Is there a New Age headquarters or a leader of the New Age?

No, there isn't. There are many New Age groups with their individual leadership structures, and they cooperate a good deal, but each one wants to be in charge, and there is no central, recognized authority. Of course, behind the scenes, they all have one "central authority" whose name is Lucifer, but most of them don't realize it.

## 4. Do they recognize Jesus as Lord?

Definitely not; like Masonry, New Agers take the usual vapid line that Jesus was a wonderful man, a "master teacher" (remember the Rainbow Girls and their burial service?), a "highly evolved avatar," and so on. But, they deny His uniqueness as "the Way, the Truth, and the Life." They, like Masonry, humanize and water down their concept of Jesus Christ, and, like Masonry, they don't seem to realize that a watered-down Jesus is no Jesus at all.

## 5. In what other ways is the New Age related to Masonry?

In doctrinal ways, they are closely related, being basically occult in their beliefs. Both teach about the "Christ Spirit," a spark of deity in everyone that merely needs to be discovered and released, the perfectibility of man, the basic goodness of man, etc. Doctrinally, Masonry and the New Age are in the same big bag. You see, the New Age, as we know it, isn't more than about one hundred years old. One of its first leaders was Madame Blavatsky, founder of the Theosophical Society. She was a close friend and frequent companion of Albert Pike, author of the ultimate Masonic classic, *Morals and Dogma*, and virtual father of modern, occult Freemasonry.[2]

## 6. What other ties, if any, are there between Masonry and the New Age?

Until a few years ago, the official journal of the Supreme Council, Thirty-third Degree, Southern Jurisdiction, by far the most influential Masonic periodical publication, was called *The New Age*. The name was changed to *Scottish Rite Journal*, apparently because of "bad press" from Christian writers and broadcasters. Masonry has in no way distanced itself from the New Age occultism and world view, but, by changing the name of the magazine, that relationship isn't so readily apparent.

## 7. Who is Alice Bailey?

During her busy lifetime, Alice Bailey was spiritual successor to Madame Blavatsky as the most prominent New Age writer and teacher of more recent times.

## 8. Was Alice Bailey in any way connected to Masonry as Madame Blavatsky was?

Yes, she was, at least in her heart and in her relationships with Masonry's "mystics," such as the late Manly P. Hall. As a matter of fact, she wrote something extremely significant about Masonry and the New Age in one of her many books. In *The Externalisation of the Hierarchy*, Mrs. Bailey wrote that there would be three primary channels for preparing the American people to receive the New Age messiah, Lord Maitrayah: the traditional ("dead") church system, the schools (educational system), and Freemasonry. She said that Masonry would be thus valuable and effective because it understands the occult principles of initiation and the mystery religions.[3] It appears that she was right.

## 9. How does all this fit in with the New World Order?

Here, again, is a rather broad, amorphous phenomenon. To try to clarify and neatly define the New World Order is like trying to stack soft jello, but we must try.

The New World Order is a generalized goal or dream of a great many powerful people, a future time when there will be a one-world government and a one-world banking system, all with an elite group in charge. Most of them also want a one-world religion, and that will be New Age paganism, the worship of nature, fertility, and sex.

Sound familiar? It should because I just described the ancient mysteries, that old wisdom religion, that old veneration of the phallus and all that goes with it.

Yes, we are back to Freemasonry and the revival it seeks; we have come full cycle.

## 10. Is Lucifer included anywhere in all this New Age/New World Order/Masonic paganism?

Absolutely, and he is there right in the middle of it all. He is clever enough to stay in the shadows (that is, after all, a natural environment for him), but he has been there all along, guiding, inspiring, orchestrating the whole thing.

## 11. Are any of Masonry's leaders worshipers of Lucifer?

Yes, of course; there are many among the "mystics" and occultists of Masonry, as a private matter of personal conviction. But, it seems also to be true that Masonic leaders at the very top (that strange, misty level of international power and influence that we might call "the illuminati" level of power) are all Luciferians and sincere ones. They believe that Lucifer is really the "good" god, that Jehovah was jealous of Lucifer's beauty and wrote a bunch of lies about him in the Bible, that someday Lucifer will come out on top, and, when he does, his followers will be with him.

## 12. What is meant by "illuminati"?

The term merely means, "the illumined, or enlightened ones," the ones who have found "the light" and, as a result, have the knowledge and wisdom to be competent to control the rest of us. They really believe that they know best what we need and think they should have the power to run it all.

## 13. Is "the Illuminati" an organization with a leader, a headquarters, etc.?

No, not as such, at least to my knowledge. In the late eighteenth century, there was such a society of European elitists organized by Adam Weishaupt in Bavaria. Their "illuminism" was well received in certain Masonic circles, spread even to America, and was a matter of great concern to George Washington, who warned the nation against it in his last years of life. Today's power brokers are Weishaupt's philosophical descendants, no doubt, but they have built their own organizations (e.g., Trilateral Commission, Council on Foreign Relations, Bilderbergers, etc.).

## 14. Do any of Masonry's leaders and writers ever come right out and admit that they serve Lucifer?

That is seldom done. We get occasional glimpses of this in their writings, but, for the most part, they have always seemed aware that it would do them more harm than good to come out in the open.

We saw the statement by Manly P. Hall in chapter 20, in which he spoke of the Mason's possessing "the seething energies of Lucifer." Albert Pike wrote, somewhat cryptically, of Satan in *Morals and Dogma,*

> Lucifer, the Light Bearer! Strange and mysterious name to give to the Spirit of Darkness! Lucifer, the Son of the Morning! Is it he who bears the light, and with its splendors intolerable blinds feeble, sensual, or selfish souls? Doubt it not![4]

This can only be described as an attempt to "set the record straight" on poor, misunderstood, maligned Lucifer.

## 15. What is Palladian Masonry, or the Palladian Rite of Masonry?

I can only say very, very little about Palladian Masonry, for there is only very, very little known about it. It may not even exist, but there are some indications of Masonic rites, above the level of the Thirty-third Degree, of the most closely kept secrecy. If they exist, their members are carefully selected from those of the highest Masonic degrees, their theology is Luciferian, and their secrecy sealed with assurance of certain death for any would-be seceder.

As I said, there may not be such a group (or groups), but, if there is, three things are certain:

1. These men would possess enormous power, both financial/political power and satanic spiritual power, the true "Maji" of which Manly P. Hall, J.D. Buck, and other occult Masonic philosophers wrote;

2. It would be virtually impossible to learn much about it, for to betray it would be to die; and,

3. Such a Masonic Rite, if it exists, is at the very center of a global conspiracy to establish the New Age and the New World Order.

## 16. Where is all this leading?

The forces of darkness are more out in the open every day. These people mean business. It appears that the end-time conflict is approaching showdown time, and we can no longer find any middle ground. I believe that we will all either be a part of the great end-time revival or of the great end-time falling away, and we no longer have any latitude for dabbling in evil.

The choice is clear. The choice is ours. The time is now.

## Endnotes

1. As a matter of fact, some years back the New Age people bought a full-page ad in the *New York Times*, announcing that he had already arrived on earth. He is yet, however, to make public appearances.

2. There is some evidence that Pike and Madame Blavatsky were lovers. They were frequently seen, arm in arm, around Washington during Pike's long tenure as Sovereign Grand Commander, Supreme Council of the Thirty-third Degree, etc.

3. A. A. Bailey, *Externalisation of the Hierarchy* (New York: Lucis Publishing Co., 1957), 510-512.

4. Albert Pike, *Morals and Dogma*, rev. ed. (Washington, DC: House of the Temple, 1950), 321.

# Appendix A

# Female "Brothers" in the Lodge

One of Freemasonry's fundamental tenets is the exclusion of women. This is one of the "Ancient Landmarks" of Masonic law. The original charges compiled by Anderson and Desaguliers, modern Masonry's founders, were explicit in this regard, saying, "the persons admitted members of a Lodge must be good and true *men*, . . . no bondmen, no women" (the emphasis on "men" is in the original).

If you ask most Masons why they don't accept women in the Lodge, they will be stumped for an answer, saying something like, "Well, uh, we just never have." If you ask one of the few who study and enquire, the justification usually given goes something like this: "Well, since speculative Masonry is based on the customs of the old operative stonemason guilds, and since their work was so strenuous, lifting and moving those big stones, women couldn't perform it, and didn't belong to their guilds. The same tradition has carried over into speculative Masonry, and that's why we don't take women into the Lodge." Both of these men, incidentally, will probably be sincere. But, the truth is probably something darker.

The true reason for Masonry's historic exclusion of women is probably much darker than most Masons suspect; the truth is probably rooted (of course) in the occult. Since the true (esoteric, hidden) meaning of Masonry's rituals and symbols is phallic, based on the ancient worship of the sun, and since its rays were thought of as phallic, penetrating the (female) earth from above and causing the earth to conceive and bring forth new life, and since the phallus is a piece of reproductive equipment God didn't issue to women, they couldn't participate in this symbolic impregnation. This being the case, a woman cannot be made a Mason, simply because a woman cannot be made a man.

There seem to have been a few bizarre exceptions to the "no women" rule. The first known was Elizabeth St. Leger (later Mrs. Richard Aldworth). As a young girl in Ireland, during Masonry's earliest days, her father and brother were members of a lodge that met in her home (other versions have it meeting in a tavern, etc.). At any rate, she overheard, one night, a meeting and its ritual, was fascinated, and listened regularly until discovered by the men. They considered killing her but decided instead to initiate her into the Entered Apprentice Degree, swearing her to secrecy, under penalty of death, with the usual oath of obligation. Portraits of her, in Masonic apron and badges, have hung in many Irish Lodge halls ever since.

There are other stories of women who became Masons, in one way or another. Henry Wilson Coil, in his *Masonic Encyclopedia*, lists a total of seven but doesn't necessarily authenticate them all. Catherine Sweet, of Kentucky, was apparently the only woman ever to be a Master Mason. Her story is similar to that of Elizabeth St. Leger in that she arranged to spy on the initiations of all three Blue Lodge Degrees, learned them "better than the men," and, when discovered, was taken in herself and "initiated, passed and raised," becoming history's only female Master Mason.

# Appendix B

## "Death Oaths"

Since the very first revelations of the secrets of Freemasonry, the oaths of obligation have been probably the number one lightning rod of negative public reaction. And, I suppose, they should be. This was true during the high tide of anti-Masonic feeling and activity during the last half of the nineteenth century, and it has been true again in the latter part of the twentieth century, during the growing public awareness of Masonry's ugly realities.

As you already know, there is one of these horrible oaths of torture, death, and mutilation for each degree. Even some of the adoptive Masonic orders for the "gentler sex" have such oaths. So, to reproduce them all, or even a tenth of them, here, would be too much for both of us. I wouldn't want to write them, and you definitely would not want to read them. (And, even if you did read them all, you would soon lose your awareness of which you were reading, for they all sound so much alike.)

Here are some of the penalty portions of commonly earned degrees. You will see the similarities, as well as the barbarity, of these "solemn obligations" imposed by this "civilizing, character-building Masonic system." You need to know that the oaths, like all the rituals, will vary in some small details from one area to another; however, they are remarkably uniform when one considers all the possibilities for modification and distortion in the lodges spread clear around the world.

• "All this I most solemnly, sincerely promise and swear, with a firm and steadfast resolution to perform the same, without any mental reservation or secret evasion of mind whatever, binding myself under no less penalty than that of having my throat cut across, my tongue torn out by its roots, and my body buried in the rough sands of the sea, at low-water mark, where the tide ebbs and flows twice in twenty-four hours, should I ever knowingly violate this, my Entered Apprentice obligation, so help me God, and keep me steadfast in the due performance of the same." (Entered Apprentice, or first, degree)

   • "Binding myself under no less penalty than that of having my breast torn open, my heart plucked out, and given as prey to the birds of the air and the beasts of the field should I ever knowingly violate this my Fellow Craft obligation. So help me . . ." (Fellow Craft, or second, degree)

   • "Binding myself under no less penalty than that of having my body severed in twain [this is just exalted Masonic wording for "cut in two"], my bowels taken from thence and burned to ashes, and scattered before the four winds of heaven . . ." (Master Mason, or third, degree)

Even that fun-loving order, the Shrine, Masonry's party boys and ambassadors of good will, participate in these graphic oaths:

> In wilful violation thereof may I incur the fearful penalty of having my eyeballs pierced to the center with a three-edged blade, my feet flayed [cut across in thin strips], and be forced to walk the hot sands upon the sterile shores of the Red Sea until the flaming sun shall strike me with livid plague . . . etc., etc. (Ancient Arabic Order, Nobles of the Mystic Shrine)

Furthermore, even the women, the so-called gentler sex, take part in these horrible oaths:

> "I further promise and vow, with a firm and steady purpose to perform and keep the same under no less penalty than having my body severed in fourteen pieces and thrown in the river, if I violate any part of this my obligation." The Commandress then directs, "You will kiss the Bible three times, the Koran once, and the Red Stone of Horus once." (Ritual, National Imperial Court of the Daughters of Isis, North and South America)

Because of growing public awareness of such bloody, atrocious death oaths, some Masonic jurisdictions are making changes, omitting the more offensive portions. Most, however, retain the "ancient" obligations, unchanged. And, even if all their oaths had the parts requiring torture, death, and mutilation removed, it wouldn't make their oaths scriptural nor change any of the basic abominations of the system.

# Appendix C

# The "Lost Word" and Its Significance

Throughout Masonic writings, rituals, lectures, and degrees, there are references to something called the "lost word." One very soon becomes aware that there must be something terribly important about this word because it figures prominently in so much of what they say, write, and do. If you read and listen, you soon get the impression that the fate of western civilization, if not the entire human race, centers in this mysterious word. And, if you really read carefully, you finally learn that, in Masonic philosophy at least, it does! Then, having learned that, you will probably want to know why.

Most simply put, the lost word is the name of God. That's right, the name of God. You probably thought there was no mystery about this since He has identified Himself plainly, elaborately, and repeatedly in the Bible. I see it this way also; but Masonry has a completely different view of the matter.

Masonry's position is that God's "true" name was once known to a select, elite priesthood in those long-ago, "good old days" when the world was pagan, the mystery religions were in full flower, and everyone happily worshiped the phallus. Then, as time went by, stupid, unenlightened, narrow-minded bigots (you guessed it, Christians, that's us) came along and, failing to appreciate the "grandeur, beauty and perfection" of all that orgiastic, sex-worshiping paganism, got rid of all of their sorcerers, magicians, and other masters of black arts who knew what the word was. And, so, the tragedy of tragedies, it was lost.

But, still you might wonder, what is such a problem because people can't remember a name? Here, in the answer to this question, is the very heart of all occultism, especially witchcraft. In basic occult philosophy (and, I might add, practice), if anyone knows the true name of a spirit, one then possesses that spirit's power and can control that spirit. The result, then, is that, knowing the name of the spirit and being able to control it, one has that spirit's power—not the power of other spirits necessarily, but the power of that one.

If, then, knowing the name of a minor spirit, wisping about some obscure neighborhood in Hometown, USA, doing dirty little deeds for Satan, would give you its power, just think what it would mean if you could know the "lost" name of God, Himself. Obviously, it would mean (if the occultists are right, which, of course, they aren't) you would then have, and be able to use, all the power of God. In fact, you could take over and become the God of the universe, yourself.

This was Lucifer's big mistake, and intelligent people the world over are going to great expense and effort trying to repeat it.

You may still be wondering how this lost word fits into Masonic philosophy and teaching. The search for the lost word is a thread running throughout Masonic degrees, teachings, and writings. Since Masonry defines itself as a search for "light," it is a search for knowledge. Since the acquisition of knowledge (enlightenment), in general (the "Lost Wisdom of the Ancients"), is the heart of the Masonic plan of redemption and since in Masonry "Initiation and Regeneration are synonymous terms" (J.D. Buck in *Mystic Masonry*, page 44), it should not be surprising that the quest to find and possess the "Grand Masonic Word," the "Ineffable Name" of God, is the centerpiece of the initiation into the Master Mason degree, the truly climactic degree in pure Freemasonry.

In the Third Degree, the initiate must participate in the reenactment of the legend of Hiram Abiff, entering into Hiram's death, burial, and resurrection. In the drama, this Hiram is the only one who knows the "Master's Word" and, with his murder by three "ruffians" (could this be a veiled reference to Trinitarian Christians and their Triune God?), the knowledge of the all-important word is lost. Truth is lost. Light is lost.

In the story, while Hiram is dead and in the grave (for three days and nights—Satan never has any original ideas), King Solomon decides that, when his body is found and restored to life, the very first thing that Hiram says will be the "substitute word."

Well, the body was found, dug up, restored to life, and raised up from the grave by Solomon with the Master Mason's grip. When Hiram was "raised" from the grave, the first thing he said was "Mah Hah Bone." This strange expression, according to the legend, then became the substitute for the real name, the true "lost word," and Masons the world over have been looking everywhere trying to recover the lost word ever since.

You may still be wondering what this all really means. Well, depending on how we view it, not much—or everything. In that it is revealing of the true, occult nature of Masonry, its very philosophical and spiritual heart, it is extremely important. In the sense that sincere Masons all over the world take this dumb story seriously and are deceived by it, it matters a very great deal. In terms of reality and truth, it is absurd.

Ever since I first read the legend of Hiram and first studied the Master Mason initiation, I have had a question for which I find no logical answer in all of Masonic lore. You have probably already thought of it, but I'll point it out anyway. If the lost word was so all-important, if it was the key to life, death, and eternity, and the doorway to happiness, and it was lost when Hiram was killed, then why, when Solomon raised him from the dead, didn't he just ask him what it was? Why fool with a substitute? Why didn't Solomon just say, "Hey, Hiram. Welcome back to the land of the living! Praise the Lord, we're glad to have you back! Now, tell us, just what was that word all this fuss has been about?"

I mean why fool around with a "substitute" word and plunge humanity into an endless spiritual darkness, searching and groping forever for the real one? Why didn't he just ask Hiram what the real word is? This pivotal moment in human history (according to Masonry's philosophers) didn't need to happen. And, for grown men, with brain enough to memorize all that childish, catechetic drivel, to take it seriously can only be described as (please forgive me if this seems harsh) stupid!

There it is, and now you know the meaning of the lost word and the story of the ongoing search for it in the Masonic Lodge.

If you would like to know more about the legend of Hiram Abiff, the lost word, or the initiation ritual of the Master Mason's degree, you will find it in the Huntington House book, *The Deadly Deception*, by this author and Jim Shaw.

# Appendix D

# Masonry and Its
# Controversial Authorities

Freemasonry has a growing problem; as a matter of fact, it is a self-compounding one. As more and more of the unflattering truth about Freemasonry is revealed, by books such as this, by preaching and teaching, by radio and television ministries, and by increasingly frequent public controversies, such as the gigantic one within the Southern Baptist Convention, ugly truth is escaping. And, once such truth, no matter how small an amount, escapes into public awareness, it spreads exponentially in all directions. As more questions are raised publicly about Masonry, interest grows, and still more questions are asked.

The cork is out of the bottle, so to speak, and Masonry can't get it back into place, let alone recover what has already escaped from the bottle.

If you have read this far in this book, names like Albert Pike, Albert Mackey, J.D. Buck, and Manly P. Hall are as familiar to you by now as those of your neighbors. But, most people, outside the highest Masonic circles, have never heard of them. As a matter of fact, most Masons have never heard of them; the books these Masonic authorities have written are on the shelf of every lodge of any size, but most Masons not only don't read them, they don't even know that they are there. Masonry's leaders like it that way because as long as the general ignorance prevails, they are not being asked awkward questions about the real meaning of what is said and done in the Lodge.

Most Masons confronted with some incriminating statement by Albert Pike are likely to look blank and reply, "Albert who?" Even Lodge secretaries, custodians of the Lodge's Masonic library, may never have read most of the Masonic classics cited in this book.

Furthermore, at Masonry's top levels of leadership, Grand Lodge level and above, it has been a traditional policy simply to remain silent when awkward or embarrassing things make the news. They know how quickly the public forgets and simply remain inconspicuous and silent while that predictable process runs its course. For a long time, it has not only worked, but has been completely sufficient. But, it isn't working these days; there is simply too much truth escaping, coming before the public, and in an ongoing way.

Now that the public (including Blue Lodge Masons!) is being educated to the truth about the secret doctrines of Masonry, acquainted with the utterances and doctrinal teachings of such Masonic standouts as Albert Pike, Albert Mackey, Joseph Fort Newton, J.D. Buck, and Manly P. Hall, these revered Masonic philosophers are becoming a problem. They are becoming an embarrassment. What are the Masonic leaders to do? They have tried two basic stratagems lately, and neither holds any water.

One defense against being confronted with the writings of their own best authorities is to say that these men don't speak for all of Masonry, that they were fringe group extremists just speaking their private, off-beat opinions.

But, you can look in any Masonic library, or catalog of Masonic books, and these men's works will be there, not just there, but prominently. Or, you can write to, or call, any Grand Lodge and tell them you are interested in a serious study of Masonry and ask for a list of ten top books or authorities; if you do, you will find those most often quoted in this book making every Mason's list.

Secondly, with more and more of the public (including some undeceived Masons who are beginning to ask questions) confronting Masonic leaders with the elitist, occult, Luciferian writings of the Masonic philosophers, there has been a tendency to disclaim them as extremists writing heresies. This boat won't float, folks, not even for a minute of clear thinking.

I can demolish this defense with just one fact, an undeniable fact, and it is this: Not one single Masonic authority, not one major leader, not one spokesman for any significant segment of Masonry has publicly denounced a single one of the Masonic authorities quoted in this book. Not a single word of public denial of any of them! If the writings and teachings of these men are unorthodox, heretical, or in any way offensive to Masonry's top leaders, they haven't spoken against a single one! This should be enough to give the lie to their denials, but the case against them gets even stronger.

Not only have these Masonic philosophers not been denounced by Masonic officialdom, they have received the highest public endorsement! I will cite just two examples and rest my case.

(1) Easily the standout Mason of the last 150 years was Albert Pike. His Masonic titles and honors alone would fill a book. His classic book *Morals and Dogma*, is perhaps the most significant Masonic book ever written. This ponderous, thousand-page tome is the ultimate source book for the "esoteric" (true, hidden) meaning of Masonic symbolism and doctrine. It is also the most closely kept, difficult of all Masonic books for the non-Mason researcher to obtain. And, since it has been obtained by some of us, it has become the one most embarrassing, hard-to-explain-away publication with which Masonry is confronted. Is Pike a fringe group wacko in the eyes of Masonry's leaders? Not a chance! If you travel to the awesome House of the Temple in Washington, D.C. ("The House that Pike Built"), headquarters of the Supreme Council of the Thirty-third Degree, etc., you will find three statues of Pike there and the Albert Pike museum. And, as a matter of fact, old Albert himself is there—buried in the wall! It took a special act of Congress in order to bury him there. In addition, the current Sovereign Grand Commander, C. Fred Kleinknecht, Pike's successor, wrote in the January 1989 *The New Age* (now published under the new title *Scottish Rite Journal*), summarizing the official view of *Morals and Dogma*: "Pike's great book is not the book of an hour, a decade or a century. It is a book for all time." Sovereign Grand Commander Kleinknecht then closed his article with this ringing declaration of support for Pike and his book: "Abandon *Morals and Dogma*? Never!"

(2) Manly Palmer Hall, Thirty-third Degree Mason, quintessential Masonic Mystic, and internationally renowned occultist, the one who wrote that the Mason "has the seething energies of

Lucifer in his hand," was not only not denounced and denied by Masonic officialdom, but rather given a glowing tribute in *The New Age/Scottish Rite Journal* following his death in 1990, with his tribute also honoring Albert Pike. It will be useful, I think, to quote from some of it here; it speaks condensed volumes:

> Illustrious Manly Palmer Hall, often called "Masonry's Greatest Philosopher," departed his earthly labors . . . August 7, 1990. . . . [He] received the Scottish Rite's highest honor, the Grand Cross, in 1985 because of his exceptional contributions to Freemasonry, the Scottish Rite and the public good. Like Grand Commander Albert Pike before him, Illustrious Hall did not teach a new doctrine, but was an ambassador of the ageless tradition of wisdom. . . . The World is a better place because of Manly Palmer Hall.

So, does Masonic officialdom deny and denounce these writers and warn Masons against their "heresies"? No, in fact, they publicly and enthusiastically endorse them. If you confront any Masons with the quotations from Masonic writers in this book, and they respond by saying that they are extremists and that high leadership has denounced them, ask them to show you the evidence. They can't for the simple reason that there isn't any.

No, the Masonic philosophers and writers of doctrine in this book are not only not renegades denied by Masonry's highest leaders, they are their most honored writers of doctrine. Don't let anyone tell you otherwise!

# Index

# More Good Books From Huntington House

## The Extermination of Christianity- A Tyranny of Consensus
*by Paul Schenck with Robert L. Schenck*

If you are a Christian, you might be shocked to discover that: Popular music, television, and motion pictures are consistently depicting you as a stooge, a hypocrite, a charlatan, a racist, an anti-Semite, or a con artist; you could be expelled from a public high school for giving Christian literature to a classmate; and you could be arrested and jailed for praying on school grounds. This book is a catalogue of anti-Christian propaganda—a record of persecution before it happens!

**ISBN 1-56384-051-0 $9.99**

## The Burning of a Strange Fire
*by Barney Fuller*

To over 7,000,000 people, Joseph Smith is the greatest of all prophets. But in *The Burning of a Strange Fire* the reader will witness that Joseph Smith is, perhaps, the greatest false prophet the world has ever seen. Most Mormons have no knowledge of the very powerful occult spirits that provided Joseph Smith with his mysterious prophetic anointing. As a former Mormon elder, Mr. Fuller takes the reader into the early life of the Mormon prophet. He reveals the most successful deception in Christian history.

**ISBN 1-56384-049-9 $9.99**

## The Dark Side of Freemasonry
### by Ed Decker

This book is probably the most significant document ever prepared on the subject of the dark side of the Masonic Lodge. In June 1993, a group of Christian researchers, teachers, and ministry leaders met in Knoxville, Tennessee, to gather together all available information on the subject of Freemasonry and its relationship to the Christian world. Ed Decker brought this explosive material back from Knoxville and here presents it as a warning to those who are unaware of the danger of the Masonic movement.

**ISBN 1-56384-061-8 $9.99**


## Conservative, American & Jewish— I Wouldn't Have It Any Other Way
### by Jacob Neusner

Neusner has fought on the front lines of the culture war and here writes reports about sectors of the battles. He has taken a consistent, conservative position in the academy, federal agencies in the humanities and the arts, and in the world of religion in general and Judaism in particular. Engaging, persuasive, controversial in the best sense, these essays set out to change minds and end up touching the hearts and souls of their readers.

**ISBN 1-56384-048-0 $9.99**


## New World Order: The Ancient Plan of Secret Societies
### by William T. Still

For thousands of years, secret societies have cultivated an ancient plan which has powerfully influenced world events. Until now, this secret plan has remained hidden from view. This book presents new evidence that a military take-over of the U.S. was considered by some in the administration of one of our recent presidents. Although averted, the forces behind it remain in secretive positions of power.

**ISBN 0-910311-64-1 $8.99**

## Kinsey, Sex and Fraud:
## The Indoctrination of a People
### by Dr. Judith A. Reisman and Edward Eichel

Kinsey, Sex and Fraud describes the research of Alfred Kinsey which shaped Western society's beliefs and understanding of the nature of human sexuality. His unchallenged conclusions are taught at every level of education—elementary, high school, and college—and quoted in textbooks as undisputed truth.

The authors clearly demonstrate that Kinsey's research involved illegal experimentations on several hundred children. The survey was carried out on a nonrepresentative group of Americans, including disproportionately large numbers of sex offenders, prostitutes, prison inmates, and exhibitionists.

**ISBN 0-910311-20-X $10.99**

## A Jewish Conservative
## Looks at Pagan America
### by Don Feder

With eloquence and insight that rival contemporary commentators and essayists of antiquity, Don Feder's pen finds his targets in the enemies of God, family, and American tradition and morality. Deftly . . . delightfully . . . the master allegorist and Titian with a typewriter brings clarity to the most complex sociological issues and invokes giggles and wry smiles from both followers and foes. Feder is Jewish to the core, and he finds in his Judaism no inconsistency with an American Judeo-Christian ethic. Questions of morality plague school administrators, district court judges, senators, congressmen, parents, and employers; they are wrestling for answers in a "changing world." Feder challenges this generation and directs inquirers to the original books of wisdom: the Torah and the Bible.

**ISBN 1-56384-036-7 Trade Paper $9.99**
**ISBN 1-56384-037-5 Hardcover $19.99**